Own It!

ALSO BY TABATHA COFFEY

It's Not Really About the Hair

Own It!

Be the Boss
of Your Life — at Home
and in the Workplace

TABATHA COFFEY

itbooks
AN IMPRINT OF HARPERCOLLINS PUBLISHERS

This book is written as a source of information only. The information contained in this book should by no means be considered a substitute for the advice, decisions, or judgment of the reader's accountant or other financial and professional adviser.

HarperCollins books may be purchased for educational, business, or sales promotional use. For information please e-mail the Special Markets Department at SPsales@harpercollins.com.

FIRST EDITION

Designed by Paula Russell Szafranski

Library of Congress Cataloging-in-Publication Data has been applied for.

ISBN 978-0-06-225100-8

14 15 16 17 18 OV/RRD 10 9 8 7 6 5 4 3 2 1

I dedicate this book to all of you,

for the support, the encouragement,

and the motivation

CONTENTS

INTRODUCTION   xi

PART I: OWN WHO YOU ARE

Chapter 1: **Attitude**   3

Chapter 2: **Passion**   19

Chapter 3: **Style**   29

PART II: OWN YOUR BUSINESS

Chapter 4: **Plan**   43

Chapter 5: **Money**   61

Chapter 6: **Brand**   75

Chapter 7: **Clients**   89

Chapter 8: **Success**   101

PART III: OWN YOUR NETWORK

Chapter 9: **Personal Relationships**   113

Chapter 10: **Work Relationships**   123

CONTENTS

PART IV: OWN YOUR CHALLENGES

Chapter 11: **Reputation**   145

Chapter 12: **Competition**   157

Chapter 13: **Decisions**   165

Chapter 14: **Mistakes**   175

Chapter 15: **Well-being**   187

Chapter 16: **Changes**   199

CONCLUSION: **Own It All!**   205

APPENDIX: **Ask Tabatha**   209

ACKNOWLEDGMENTS   237

Own It!

INTRODUCTION

I'm Tabatha. I'm tough . . . I'm talented . . . and I teach people to take the reins and cut the bullshit. Some call what I do "tough love." You better believe it is. I have made grown men cry like babies. But they thanked me later. Why? Because I taught them how to Own It.

"Owning it" means taking responsibility for your actions, your words, your decisions, your failures, your successes, and ultimately your life and your destiny. If your career, your business, or your relationship is failing, then you need to figure out how to change yourself to fix the problems. Don't make excuses or blame everyone around you. Own the fact that every part of your life belongs to you and is affected by how you think and act.

I like to make this comparison: one day, I was eating dinner in a restaurant, and a mother and her young son were sitting at the table next to me. The kid was throwing breadsticks, and the mom was just sitting there, sipping her glass of wine, allowing it to happen. Food was flying all over the restaurant while people were trying to enjoy their meals.

"He's working through a phase," she explained with a smile as a breadstick soared over my head.

I bit my tongue (which is hard for me, we all know how direct I am), but what I wanted to say was: "I have a very simple solution to work through that phase. Tell your child 'Put the breadstick down right now or we are leaving.'"

It made me furious that the mother was not taking any responsibility for her ill-mannered child. And yet I see this situation all the time. It's a fucking epidemic: people shirking responsibility, burying their heads in the sand, pointing the finger of blame at everyone else, and not wanting to take control of a difficult situation. Some people don't want to admit that *they* are the problem. They refuse to Own It.

A lot of people write to me asking for advice and help. I get questions about everything from how to style hair (I have thirty-two years in the hair industry under my belt) and where I get my clothes (my little secret!), to how to deal with credit card debt, bossy spouses, and the fucking idiots they work with. I decided to write this book because I enjoy helping people, and because I think the world would be a better place if we all took more responsibility for ourselves and our lives. On my Bravo show *Tabatha Takes Over*, I've taken over countless businesses and shown them the error of their ways. Most of them heed my advice, and I'm often impressed when I go back six weeks or six months later and see how they have improved their profits and how happy their staff and customers are. A few don't listen to me . . . and they're out of business. Check out the Q&A section at the end of the book for my answers to some of the common business questions that I've received.

Although every business I advise is different and their problems are somewhat unique, the one thing they all have in common is the approach I bring to solving their problems. I've learned never to sugarcoat things. You need to be honest, direct, and sometimes blunt about what is going on in a situation if you really want to change it and build success. Change is hard, and a lot of people would prefer to sit comfortably in misery and routine than deal with the hard work of boat rocking that needs to happen. Most of the businesses I go into need a head-to-toe overhaul; things have gone from bad to shit, and now there is no alternative but for me to come in and close everything down for a week, tear the place apart, teach everyone to behave like grown-ups, and start over. I use tough love because I have very little time and I don't tolerate attitude, excuses, lateness, or laziness. I observe, inspect, and meet with everyone involved to get all sides of the story. Then, when I've seen enough, I take the owners' keys away as a symbol of power. They don't get them back until I see they have started to make the changes needed and they are owning it.

In the case of this book, you will have to assess for yourself when you are ready and deserving of your keys. So imagine that right now I am taking them. They are mine for the next sixteen chapters. And when you feel like you are ready and able to own your life, you will take them back and use them to open yourself up to great success. Your success is my success, so we're in this together.

I believe my approach to owning it isn't just about helping businesses and their owners. It is applicable to everything in life, from relationships to child rearing. My approach comes from years of personal experience, which I'll be sharing with you. A few things I know for certain: goals will change. Circumstances will change. People will come and go in your life, and they will surprise you and sometimes disappoint you. But you never have to let things just "happen" to you. You have the power to take control of your situation and make of it what you want. No situation is ever hopeless and you're never helpless. I want every person who reads this book to face the most difficult situations in his or her life with the ability to own it.

And when you do, I can't wait to sit next to you and your kids at dinner in a restaurant.

PART I

OWN WHO YOU ARE

Attitude

"So, people like to call me a bitch. Let's just lay it out there on the table. I am who I am and I own it. I don't suffer fools and I have no problem saying what's on my mind."

I don't do hugs. Neither did my mother, Norma—especially when it came to her business. Hugs were for a child who fell down, not for the staff at the transsexual strip clubs she ran in Australia. They thought she was tough and unforgiving. They even called her "the Nazi" (as politically incorrect as that is!) because she was so intimidating and strict. But her demands really weren't unreasonable. In a culture that was very flamboyant, she called people out on their bullshit and held them to their responsibilities. She believed in telling people what she really thought and expected, and she held them to it.

As I became a business owner, I was very concerned about being characterized the same way. But I knew that my mother had amazing leadership qualities, which I wanted to emulate. She ran her clubs smoothly and efficiently. Fast-forward a few years to *Shear Genius* on Bravo, a reality show that pits hairstylists from all walks of life against each other. I was one of those stylists on Season 1. Viewers came to know me as a fierce competitor who had a passion for my craft and who shared my opinions and was honest. How honest? *Brutally* honest. If you're cutting people's hair with hedge trimmers, I am going to call you a fucking idiot. As a result, I came off like a hard-ass and became the contestant viewers loved to hate. I could deal with that—it's a competition after all. But as the season aired and I started to read the blogs and press for the show, I realized a lot of people were calling me a bitch. They even did it to my face: I was in the mall one day and a woman came up to me and said, "Hey, aren't you that bitch from TV?"

I have to say, the word was cutting and unsettling. Then I sat down and really thought hard about it. They were calling me a bitch not because they disliked me, but because I was candid and outspoken, just like my mother. *Bitch* wasn't necessarily a negative assessment of who I was—but it felt like one because the label was so one-dimensional. So I decided it was time to give *bitch* an overhaul and empower myself by removing the word's negativity. I needed to literally reinvent it and come up with a new acronym that removed the stigma and suited the person I really am:

Brave

Intelligent

Tenacious

Creative

Honest

Now being a bitch is not only *my* thing, it's a good thing. People all over tell me how empowered they feel by the word. Sometimes you need to own a word or a situation that is bringing you down. Take it and spin it on its head so that you can make it a positive experience. People still accuse me of being a bitch when I am stating an opinion—albeit a strong one. To me, *bitch* is now a compliment, and I'm proud to be one.

But just because I'm a bitch doesn't mean I have a negative attitude. If I did, I wouldn't be in the line of business I'm in (helping people). People who have a negative attitude can't get out of their own way because they see everything through a pessimistic filter. I truly see the good or potential good in most people, and I feel that any situation can be rectified with hard work and a change of perception. In fact, I'm a pretty optimistic person who looks for solutions rather than throwing in the towel.

The key is not to confuse someone's personality with his or her attitude toward life. This goes back to the old adage of not judging a book by its cover. And sometimes we are too quick to judge someone by first impressions. How many times have you met someone who was quiet and thought to yourself, She thinks she's better than me, when in fact the person was just shy and took a while to warm up?

Personality is who you are. Attitude is how you represent those traits outwardly. I'm tough, but if you've worked with me, you probably know my bark is much worse than my bite. I have learned over the years to keep my cool and stay professional at all times. When I'm in a business setting, I may be thinking to myself, You are a fucking moron, but I (usually!) don't say it. One of my attitude adjustments was learning how to self-edit. There are better, more constructive ways for me to show and tell people what they're doing wrong. On *Shear Genius* I was under constant pressure to win a challenge, so I often let my feelings bubble to the surface. But as a leader and mentor, I choose to take a different approach—and you can, too.

Most people's attitudes are developed over time as reactions to relationships and situations that may have nothing to do with the moment they are in. As I mentioned, my childhood was quite unorthodox and my mother ran a tight ship, so it's no wonder that I wound up tough as nails. Many things affect your attitude: your history, your beliefs, your emotions, even your thought patterns. All of us have emotional triggers—things that simply set us off and put us in a bad mood. One of the things that puts me in a bad mood is bad customer service. When someone doesn't care about doing a good job, I ask myself, Am I going to let this person win and ruin my day?

Sometimes you're aware of your attitude, and sometimes you're not. I've met many business owners who told me they never berated a customer or employee. Yet when I show them an actual video, there they are, ripping someone a new one. A bad attitude may indicate that you are not just antagonistic but also . . .

lazy	unaware
irresponsible	uncooperative
insecure	jealous
insincere	suspicious

A good attitude, on the other hand, shows that you are . . .

confident	genuine
compassionate	gracious
courteous	hardworking
cooperative	humble
generous	

Mind Your Own Business: Do I have an attitude problem?

In every chapter, you'll find these Mind Your Own Business features. Whenever you see them, I want you to roll up your sleeves and get busy. On my show, I put the staff and owners to work, doing everything from making burgers to cleaning a farm. Why? To prove a point and teach a lesson. Owning it takes work. These little assignments will give you the kick in the butt you need. I'm not going to know if you skip over these . . . but *you* will. And remember, you need to earn those keys back!

Many experts will say that a good attitude is what determines how successful we are in life. And a lot of leaders more spiritual than I will tell you that we get back the energy we put out. So how do you measure up? Answer the following honestly then check your answers below.

1. *The cabdriver misses your stop by a few blocks. You:*

   A. tell him he needs to have his vision checked and stiff him on a tip.

   B. say "that's okay" and seize the opportunity to get a little exercise and walk.

2. *Your boss assigns you to a group project. You:*

   A. sulk all morning. You'd much rather work by yourself than with a group of idiots.

   B. look at it as an opportunity to get to know your coworkers better and share ideas.

3. *Your boyfriend buys you a pair of fuzzy bunny slippers for your birthday. You:*

   A. take it as a sign he has "cold feet" in the relationship. If he loved you, he'd buy you jewelry.

   B. remind yourself that it's the thought that counts and he was sweet enough to remember.

4. *Your friend leaves you a message canceling dinner at the last minute. You:*

   A. write her a nasty e-mail. How dare she ditch you like this?

   B. embrace the chance to stay home, relax, and catch up on your fave TV shows.

5. *You lose your phone, spill coffee on your blouse, and get a bad haircut . . . all in one week. You:*

   A. see it as a message from the universe: life sucks and your luck sucks worse.

   B. tell yourself next week is bound to be better (it can't be worse!).

If you answered *mostly a*'s. Wow. You make me look warm and fuzzy. Why the chip on your shoulder? Your attitude is not going to get you anywhere (except on everyone's shit list). I recommend you look closely and think carefully about your reactions. Maybe keep a list of problems you encountered during the day and how you can handle them better/differently.

If you answered *mostly b*'s. Congratulations. You are grace under fire. A positive attitude like yours will not only keep you sane, but it will also make those around you more comfortable and able to cope. A word of caution: just because you like to look on the bright side doesn't mean you should put on blinders. Sometimes situations are not as rosy as they seem. Be smart and aware. You can have a good attitude while being pragmatic.

Building a better attitude

I am not going to tell you to cut the 'tude. If you want to go through life feeling like crap with a huge chip on your shoulder, then by all means, be my guest. Just steer clear of me. I have no tolerance for these types. I find more often than not such people are overcompensating for a lack of self-esteem or common sense. Where do you think this nasty or negative attitude is going to get you? Do you think it will make people want to work with you or hang out with you? The way I see it, if your attitude is holding you back and preventing you from succeeding, it needs to change.

Step 1: Look at what's causing your negative attitude.

Your feelings and emotions affect your attitude. How do you react to things? Are you calm and collected—or are you so antsy and ornery that anything can set you off? Guess what? You and only you control this. No one can *make* you pissed, depressed, or act like Attila the Hun. No one is holding a gun to your head and telling you to be a badass or a cry baby. You need to work through those emotional issues that are causing your bad attitude.

Again, bad attitudes are contagious. If the people closest to us, including family, friends, and coworkers, have negative attitudes, you may "catch" one as well. Just remember, you don't have to get upset if someone is trying to make you upset. You can choose to stay happy and upbeat. I like to think of this as wearing a bulletproof vest. People can fire negativity at me all they want (and when I do a Takeover, many of them do!). But if you remember that it is their issue, not yours, it should bounce right off you.

Sometimes your entire environment is negative. I knew a woman who worked as an editor for a small magazine. Her boss was about to be replaced, and she knew it. As a result, the boss berated everyone and went on daily tirades about what a crappy company it was to work for. The editor refused to take the bait. She kept a positive attitude and did her work to the best of her abilities. When the dust settled (and the boss was let go) management handed her the boss's position. Why? Because when everyone around her was whining, complaining, or talking shit, she was acting like a pro. Lesson learned: even if the people around you have all turned to the Dark Side and are trying to suck you into the void, you don't have to go there. This is when you go back and recall what I taught you about your vision and plan. Own both, stay on your path, and you'll keep above the fray.

Step 2: Know what needs to be changed.

Are there parts of your attitude that are doing you more harm than good? Consider how you interact with people in your life. Are there any instances when you are not getting through to them? Are your words making the problem better or bigger? As a rule of thumb, I recommend you always think before you react. I call it the three-second rule. Take a deep breath, count to three, and consider what you are about to do or say. A quick cooldown will help you see things more clearly and, more important, say what you mean instead of something heated and reactionary. Usually all it takes is three seconds—in some instances longer may be advisable. And sometimes there isn't enough time in the world, and in those instances you can't censor yourself.

Not long after my mother passed away, I was working in New Orleans. It was a rough trip for me because not only was I mourning, but I also was in our favorite city. My mum and I would visit there every year, so it had a lot of meaning for me. I decided to fly in early to visit a few of our favorite places and pay homage to her. I was in church, lighting a candle and having a moment to myself, when out of the corner of my eye, I noticed a flash that was constantly going off in my face. I looked over, and a woman was sitting in a pew with her phone aimed at me, taking pictures. I applied my three-second rule (I was, after all, in church), and then I walked over and demanded she delete all the pictures. I refrained from saying everything I wanted to, but ultimately I probably had a "bad attitude" because I felt the situation warranted it.

We are all going to experience those bad days and have to find the best way we can to let it go and move on. But if you know what your triggers are, it's that much easier to prepare yourself to handle them and to own your attitude.

CASE STUDY
The stylist with the no-can-do 'tude

I worked with a stylist who had the crappiest attitude I have ever encountered. I thought it was just reserved for me, but her workmates and boss confirmed that she was always hostile to them as well. When a client came in and asked for something, she'd refuse it with little or no explanation. She was going to do what she wanted to do—take it or leave it. The more I worked with her, the more frustrated I became. I realized that every interaction she had, whether with me, a client, or a coworker, left people frustrated and annoyed. She had a bad attitude that was contagious! Because she was treating people badly, they in turn treated her badly. It was a vicious cycle. The owners of the salon talked to her, as did I, but her attitude didn't change, and it was bringing down the team and losing clients for the salon. We all knew what had to happen: Miss Attitude Problem had to go. Interestingly, several months after the stylist had moved on to a new job, I received an e-mail from her thanking me. She told me she had been going through some personal issues and was having a difficult time dealing with them. She didn't realize how bad it had become and how much it was affecting everything she did, until she got fired. Losing her job was a wake-up call that made her reevaluate and change.

Step 3: Commit to it.

If your goal is to treat people with more patience and respect, then do it. Set a clear plan, step by step if you have to, of how and when you will do this. There will be tough days or tough situations where it will feel difficult not to slip back into your old patterns of behavior. You have to be vigilant and really own your new attitude. Changing your attitude isn't simply reciting a platitude like, "Today I'm going to see the glass as half full." It's recognizing situations that drive you in the wrong direction and putting on the breaks to turn around. It's not easy to do this. It means breaking old patterns and habits that you might be used to. But when you exude a good attitude, people are more open and receptive to your ideas. I always say you get back what you put out there.

Your attitude at work

I don't care where you are on the ladder—the top or the bottom rung. Bringing your personal problems to work is unacceptable. You need to be able to separate your professional and your personal life, and check the 'tude at the door. Your boss and coworkers don't want to hear your sob story (even if they lend a sympathetic ear, trust me—they don't!). You may not be the bad apple, but you should be aware of the people who are. A bad attitude doesn't always present itself as an employee mouthing off. It can also show up as laziness, tardiness, rumor-spreading, and "shit-stirring"—basically, anything that torpedoes morale. Negative attitudes are toxic. And once you let them in they can spread like wildfire. You'll learn in later chapters how to own your relationships with coworkers and bosses, but for now, watch out for . . .

- Low self-esteem. If workers don't feel appreciated, their attitude can take a nosedive. A little praise goes a long way.

- Boredom. Doing the same thing, day after day, is bound to make anyone cranky. Mix it up; offer opportunities to train and broaden skills and services. A person who washes hair and does little else is going to turn into a mindless zombie if you don't pay attention. Everyone needs to feel they are challenged and progressing.

- Lack of respect—for each other and for authority. You're a team, and there must be mutual respect and support. You can't just demand it; you have to earn it. Resentments brew up quickly and easily. Make sure that everyone pulls their own weight and treats each other the way they would want to be treated.

• **Not understanding mission/goals.** If no one has a clue as to what the "big picture" goals are, then you feel lost and detached. Make sure everyone is on the same page.

CASE STUDY
The boss who was impossible to please

A business owner will face a lot of trying situations. Finances may be tight, staff may let you down, and customers may be rude. But you cannot let these circumstances change your attitude toward your business or the people in it, especially toward those who haven't done anything wrong. I worked with an owner in Florida with the worst attitude I may have ever encountered. Nothing was right, nobody was good enough, and she let her staff and, at times, her clients know it. Her negative attitude affected everything her staff did or didn't do. Knowing they couldn't please her no matter what they did, they began to harbor bad attitudes as well. I had hoped that a little tough love and showing the owner how her attitude was impacting her staff and business would help. I had her staff act out the things she would say and the way she behaved.

Amazingly, she just sat there and didn't get it. She thought they were exaggerating and making it all up! She took no responsibility and continued to keep dishing it out. I wanted to get through to her and even showed her negative reviews from clients who had commented, "If I complain, she calls me up and gives me attitude!" Unfortunately I couldn't get through to her. She even gave me attitude when I renovated her salon because she didn't get *exactly* what she wanted! Some people refuse to adjust their attitude. In this case, I assume ego and deep-rooted insecurity and fear were preventing her from doing so. When this happens, I'm sorry to say that I can't help. A bad attitude can be changed only if the person willing to change.

Can a good attitude be a bad thing?

It can . . . if it prevents you from seeing the true situation at hand. I worked with an owner in California. He had a Pollyanna attitude, and it was ruining his business. His staff treated him like a doormat because he was acting like one. All he wanted was to be liked, and that is not leadership. When I asked him why his salon was failing, he assured me, "There are no problems! I just need more customers." In his mind, all he needed was more clients. He didn't see that he was as much the problem as the lack of clientele. He acted like a gopher rather than a boss. He actually got his staff lunch, cleaned up behind them, and ran their errands—all with a dopey smile on his face! He kept telling me that because he had a positive attitude, things would get better. But his attitude was doing nothing to improve the situation. A positive attitude is great, but you also need positive action. Without it, you're just making a wish—and that's not going to save your business.

Clearly, he was afraid of being "the bad guy." He didn't want his staff or clients to not like him for pointing out what was wrong. No one likes to be criticized, so yes, they may not love you if you call them out. But let's be clear: you can't let people walk all over you because you crave acceptance. This isn't a popularity contest; it's a business. I made him tell his staff what to do and taught him how to say no. The lesson I wanted to get across is that you can be authoritative and tough without being mean and rude. Like everything in business and life, it's a delicate balance.

If being positive all the time prevents you (as in this owner's case) from seeing what's wrong and leads to people walking all over you, then it's a liability. The same is true if your happy-go-lucky attitude doesn't allow you to plan for the future. You can't simply trust that things will fall into your lap. You have to do something rather than wait for something to happen to you.

- Be positive . . . not stupid. I don't believe in miracles—I believe in action. If you see something bad happening, don't allow it to happen because you trust the universe. This is being ignorant and naïve.

- Ditch your delusions. It's nice to think that you're a good person and good people deserve to succeed. In my book, you deserve to succeed if you bust your ass for it. Dream big, but put plans behind those dreams if you want them to become reality.

- Don't assume anything. Just because something worked before doesn't mean it's working now. You can't rely on what once was. You have to deal with the here and now.

- A little bit of anxiety won't kill you. You don't always have to be carefree. Worrying may heighten your awareness of a situation and point out the small problems before they become huge ones.

Norma's Notes: PICK YOURSELF UP

My mother always believed in herself, and I am sure that is what got her through many tough times. She was a positive person by nature, and she never dwelled on the negative. Her motto was: when life knocks you down get up and dust yourself off. My mother had a strong faith and a strong sense of self, and she had no time or desire to wallow in self-pity or negativity. She believed in taking charge, changing what didn't work, and getting on with life. There were many times when I would complain about situations, my mother's response would be: "It could be worse. You could be pushing up daisies."

Tabatha's Final Take: Own Your Attitude

I hate to repeat myself, so think of this "final take" section at the end of each chapter as a short and sweet study guide to reinforce what you've learned on the previous pages. Turn to it when you need a quick refresher or you're feeling less than confident. We all have those moments. Put these principles into action every day: don't just file them away. Walk the walk as well as talk the talk. Be brave and bold with your choices and stand by them.

* Personality is who you are. Attitude is how you represent those traits outwardly. You can be a tough bitch (like me) and still project a positive attitude.

* If your attitude is holding you back and preventing you from connecting with others, it's time for a change.

* A bad attitude can only be changed when someone is willing to change.

* Bad attitudes are often the result of ancient history. Don't allow your baggage to weigh you down.

* Be wary of toxic types. Their bad attitudes can be "contagious."

* Be positive . . . not stupid. A good attitude doesn't mean you stick your head up your ass and ignore the truth.

2

Passion

"When I was a kid, I would go to the salon in Australia with my mum every week. The smells of the hair lacquer, perm solution, bleach, and setting lotions were intoxicating to me, but the thing I loved most was the sense of community. It was a social gathering as much as a service. I loved watching the women walk in one way and leave completely transformed. They not only looked different, but they also felt different. They stood up straighter, had a twinkle in their eye and a glow that wasn't there before. That's what I fell in love with . . . that's what I knew I wanted to do."

When I decided to become a salon owner, it was out of frustration. That is not necessarily a good thing, but it's a valuable lesson for anyone working for someone else. I had an opinion about everything and truly believed I could run things better. But as an employee, even one in a management role, I understood that I couldn't just change whatever I wanted. I had a boss. At a certain point, my frustration at this situation fueled my desire to open my own salon. So I did. In my case, I had done the work and was ready to take this step—something this book will help you prepare for. Looking back, I see clearly how it all started. It began with a passion.

I'm lucky—I've always had a clear picture of what I wanted to do with my life. I knew I wanted to be a hairdresser from the time I was a little girl. Growing up, I spent a lot of time backstage in my parents' strip clubs, watching the dancers get ready and transform themselves. These were men who lived as women; back then they called them drag queens. Today they would be known as transsexuals. It was something straight out of *La Cage aux Folles*: sequins, feathers, eyelashes, hairpieces. It was all so glamorous. As a child, I would watch the girls come in and spend hours and hours backstage getting ready. The last step was always the wig: it completed the look and made them become the person they wanted to be. The glamorous makeup and costumes were nothing without the hair.

Eventually I learned to style their wigs and bead their costumes. They changed their outside appearances to transform themselves into how they felt on the inside, and I knew that I wanted a profession that would help people feel that transformation.

By the time I was fourteen, I already had my first job in a hair salon. I didn't like school and I didn't fit in. I was incredibly stubborn and tenacious even back then, and when I told my mother I wanted to be a hairdresser and leave school, she had a smart solution. Find a salon and be a Saturday girl. Saturday girls were kids who came in on the weekend (when it was busiest) and swept the floors, washed towels, and cleaned. I found a place that said they would take me on, but they wouldn't pay me. "Fine," I told them. "I'll work for free." That's how badly I wanted to be a hairdresser, and that's how much I wanted to prove it to my mum. I worked after school, on weekends, and all through my school holidays for no pay for just over a year because I loved it. They couldn't get rid of me! Even when my bosses would tell me to go home, I would stay and watch. I didn't want to miss out on anything. I was mesmerized as I watched men and women cut, color, and style hair. I wanted to do it all . . . and better.

One of my favorite aspects of being a hairdresser is education and hair shows. Being onstage demonstrating new techniques and looks on a platform and educating others was a rush. Every time I went onstage, I felt like a rock star. That adrenaline rush confirmed for me that this was what I was meant to be doing. So I let my passion fuel my goals and plans. Those plans evolved over the years, but the passion is what is always behind it. I went from a stylist to a salon owner to a TV personality and motivational speaker. I believe you should always challenge yourself and stretch beyond your comfort zone—it's how we grow. When doors open, you have to be brave enough to walk through them.

But not everyone knows what they want to be when they grow up. Maybe you have no clue. Or maybe you're in a line of work that isn't satisfying and you're ready for a change. Or maybe you once had a passion and lost it, and now it needs rekindling. Ultimately, you need to be excited to get out of bed in the morning. If you're dragging your butt and dreading the alarm clock, you're not in the right business. You have to love what you do—not just put up with it. I meet a lot of business owners who never had passion and yet they can't figure out why their staff and/or their clientele doesn't give a shit. I'll tell you why: you lead by example. If you're bored, pissed off, or simply going through the motions, how do you think you're going to make everyone around you feel? When I see a boss who is passionless, I know exactly why his or her business is tanking.

I also meet a lot of people who once had a passion and let it slip away. I suggest a little exercise anytime someone tells me the thrill is gone—or they just have no idea where to find it. For a moment, I want you to be self-centered enough to ask yourself these most basic questions: What excites you? What makes you happy? What would you do if you could do anything? This is where your passion lies. Listen to your heart, not your head. Everyone has a passion.

Mind Your Own Business:
Connect with your passion

To get in touch with your passion, I recommend answering these questions. Remember that a passion can be as broad or as fine-tuned as you feel it. For me, my passion is twofold: hair and people. Hair is the vehicle that expresses my creativity. But I love making people feel good about themselves and empowered. For you, passion may be baking pies, designing clothes, cooking, or helping those in need. Start there. We'll work together to grow it into something that can make you money. The important thing right now is to identify where your passions lie.

Get out a pen and some paper and start writing. Something might just leap out at you and jump-start your plans.

1. What am I meant to be doing? Is there a mission/ goal you have always wanted to achieve but have let distractions and excuses keep you from it? What inspires and motivates you? What do you love to do even though you aren't getting paid for it?

2. What do I dream about? It can be as simple as making your own jewelry or as vast as building a hotel empire. Everyone has a dream, but many people see a dream as just that—something that isn't real. Every big success

story starts with a dream, but you have to believe it is actually possible.

3. What do I do well? Where do your talents lie? It doesn't have to be something you studied in school. Are you a whiz with a sewing machine? An expert at fixing things? What business/career requires these skills? Is there something you could be doing with your natural gifts?

4. How would my friends describe me? Ask them. Sometimes on the show, I can see someone far better than they see themselves and point out their strengths and weaknesses. Ask the people who know you best where they think your strengths lie.

5. What would I do if I had the money? Let's say you won the lottery and there is nothing standing in your way. What would you do with the money? Is there a way to do it anyway, either on a shoestring budget or by raising the capital?

CASE STUDY
The salon genius who thought he was a footballer

Vidal Sassoon—the man who pioneered the bob style and revolutionized the hair industry—had no aspirations of going into this line of work. He wanted to be a football player (or as Americans call it, a soccer player). But when he was fourteen, he needed to leave school and find work to help support his family. First, he was a wartime messenger—but his mother didn't think the job was suitable. So she told him she had a premonition that he should work as a hairdresser, and she arranged for him to apprentice in Cohen's Beauty Salon in London. He wasn't happy about it at first, but he eventually realized he had a great passion for hair. That passion became his vision for precision cutting, and he revolutionized an industry.

Mind Your Own Business: **Is my passion a moneymaker?**

Let's be brutally honest here. Have you asked yourself this question? I don't want to rain on anyone's parade, but sometimes your passion is not business-ready. It's relaxing for you, a haven for you, but it's a hobby . . . not a viable source of income. Just because you like to knit scarves doesn't mean you can open a knitting shop in your town. Not every person who enjoys baking pies can own a successful bakery. Consider ...

* Have I researched the market?
* Is there a demand for this service? Will people be banging down the door to get in?
* Am I tapping into a hot trend/interest?
* Is my passion something that can be organized and carried on as a business?
* Can I support myself doing this all day, every day?

I meet a lot of people who think they can turn a hobby into a business, but they are being naïve. You need to consider how you can monetize it and grow it. A business is not something you take lightly—which is why I spend so much time in this book teaching you how to Own Your Business. You need to ask tough questions so you can distinguish between the passion that you can enjoy in your spare time and the passion that can be a career. There's nothing wrong with having several passions, one that supports you and others that you enjoy because they relax you. But you need to learn the difference between them.

Not everyone is a fan

This goes without saying, but I'm going to say it: you and only you know what you are meant to be and do. A lot of people may think and tell you otherwise. Let them. You're excited and enthusiastic, so naturally you want to share your news with everyone. Just be wary that you are opening yourself up to scrutiny. Choose whom you share your passion and your dreams with. Steer clear of the toxic types who want to see you fall flat on your face. They may include:

The Nervous Nellie

She's afraid you're making a big—make that HUMUNGOUS— mistake. She is convinced that nothing good can come of this idea. She has a million reasons why it won't work and can quote you stats on how many businesses like yours fail. Say "thank you for your concern" . . . and move on. But, Tabatha, you say, she's a good friend. She means well! Sometimes, if a friend is bringing you down, you need to cut the cord. I had a salon owner who put her BFF in to manage the place so she could tend to her photography business. This so-called bestie was bad-mouthing the owner behind her back, not to mention bullying her and the entire staff. Finally the woman wised up and told her friend to take a hike. Smartest decision she ever made! A real friend supports your dream; she doesn't try to destroy it.

The Jealous Joe

He will dissuade you because the idea of you being successful would shine light on the fact that he's a total loser. He may be sneaky in his tactics, planting seeds of doubt in your mind instead of admitting he's green with envy. Take his word with a grain of salt. Or simply tell him to piss off.

The Blowhard

She has been around the block and is an expert in all things. How do you know? Because she told you so! This type will delight in pointing out what you're doing wrong ("everything") and what you're doing right ("nothing"). Ignore the FIGJAM (Fuck I'm good just ask me) and go with your gut.

Norma's Notes: HOW TO HANDLE A HATER

My mother always kept her friends close and her enemies closer. She ran a fairly scandalous business, so she kept a low profile and quietly handled anything that could be construed as "bad PR." And she understood that sometimes she needed to engage with her haters so that she knew their position and their next moves. My mother knew it was better for her to deal with an enemy than have that person go to the police or the press.

Tabatha's Final Take: Own Your Passion

✳ You don't have to be born knowing what you want to do or be. You can try things on for size. You can experiment and see what you're passionate about. When you figure it out, it's like being struck by lightning. Keep at it, and I promise you, that aha moment will arrive.

❋ Once you find your passion, don't let anyone put a damper on it. Plenty will try. (Ever notice how some people hate to see you happy?) You have to be prepared to stand strong and differentiate between helpful feedback and negative criticism.

❋ Keep an open mind. Your passion can lead you onto many different paths. Be objective and flexible, so you can expand and transform what you love into a clear vision for a business.

Style

3

"The tougher the problem, the higher the heels. Whenever I need to face a difficult situation I slip into my tallest Louboutins. Yes, they give me the height to tower over my adversaries. But that isn't the only reason I choose a high heel. The shoes empower me because they make me feel good about myself. They make me feel not just tall but also beautiful and fierce. Mind you, heels don't have to cost a thousand dollars to make you feel this way. Anyone can find shoes or clothing that gives them that 'edge' and upper hand. It's all about owning your style."

Not long ago I went to a salon to do a Takeover. I lined up the staff and began to read them the riot act. But one employee kept staring at me—he didn't seem at all fazed by what I was saying. "Are you listening?" I asked him.

"I just cannot get over that jacket," he replied, eyeing my leather Alexander McQueen peplum jacket. I swear, the young man was so obsessed he couldn't focus on what I was saying.

I am not sure why people have such a strong reaction to my "look." Perhaps it's because my style conveys my personality and it has a point of view. When I wear over-the-top theatrical pieces or bondage-inspired dominatrix looks, it's because I want to feel empowered and like a badass. What I choose to wear always reflects how I am feeling at the moment and what I know I need to deal with that day. I wear my clothes; they don't wear me. This didn't happen overnight. It came from years of me trying things, making bad fashion choices, and discovering what I like and what I didn't like. What I wore ten or fifteen years ago I wouldn't be caught dead in today, because my sense of myself has evolved and my fashion has evolved with it.

My regard for fashion has always been a guiding force. For me, fashion is highly personal. I struggled in my youth with being "the fat kid" and trying to create a style that made me feel good about myself in spite of my weight. I couldn't always fit into the "latest trend" or fad, but I could always take the "essence" of what it was and make it mine. I found inspiration in old movies or rifling through vintage stores. Maybe no one else was wearing what I was, but I have never minded standing out in a crowd.

That is probably what drew me to the rebel punk culture in London during my early career as a young hairdresser. I adopted the style of a punk rock star rebel, including wearing Doc Martens and having a shaved head. Eventually, as my career matured, so did my sense of style. I now embrace designers who are very edgy and couture, such as Alexander McQueen. I also decided some time ago that black was my signature. This isn't to say I don't see pieces that are colorful or patterned and think, I love that. But I don't choose it for myself. I save the hot pink for my pajamas.

CASE STUDY
My brush with fashion greatness

Even when I was a small child, I was always desperate to get my hands on a copy of *Vogue Paris*. I could name every designer—they were my celebrities. Same goes for today. I know more about these fashion visionaries and their collections than I do Kimmie K (no disrespect).

So you can imagine that when I finally got to meet one of my style icons for the first time, I was awestruck. I met Karl Lagerfeld at Charles de Gaulle Airport in Paris when I was in my early twenties. There was an air traffic control strike, so the flights were all delayed. He came up behind me in the check-in line and asked me (in French) what was going on. I turned and saw a skycap with a giant cart of Louis Vuitton luggage. Then I realized who the luggage belonged to. I tried to act nonchalant and cool as I answered him in English. He said something to the skycap and walked off to have a cigarette. I almost collapsed into my mother, who didn't recognize him but understood my reaction. I had been face-to-face with one of the people who helped me define myself!

When I met Jean Paul Gaultier in the early 1980s, he wasn't yet a giant global name in fashion, but I knew who he was because I had already fallen in love with his irreverent designs. I spotted him as he was walking through Camden Market in London and went over to tell him that I thought his work was brilliant. He thanked me and we parted. That was that. But even if it was only a few seconds, it was thrilling to be able to tell him what he did for me.

Honing and owning your style

Some people are born fashionistas. They instinctively know what looks good on them and others. They exude confidence and the ability to mix, match, and make things work together. They can feel it; they have a sixth sense for style. I want you to understand that you probably will not walk away from reading this chapter with a solid definition of your style. But you will be on your way, and this is an evolutionary process. Nothing stays the same, and if it does . . . well, we have all cringed at our grandfather for wearing his favorite shirt from another decade to the family brunch. I certainly have the photo album to support my evolution. Allow yourself the time and patience to find a look that works for you and makes you feel attractive, powerful, and confident. Consider:

- **Your age.** Looking youthful is one thing, but pigtails and barrettes on a thirty-year-old are infantile. Your style should reflect how far you've come (and that's beyond the sixth grade). Grow up!

- **Your job.** Let your profession be your guide when you go out shopping. I know there are plenty of creative fields where anything goes in the workplace. But there are also many situations where you need to dress like you give a shit. I am livid when I walk into a Takeover and see the stylists in ripped jeans or ratty T-shirts. How the hell are you going to make me look good if you can't brush your own hair or find something that's not wrinkled to put on? A little polish goes a long way.

- **Your life.** Fashion should combine form and function and make sense for your surroundings. If you live in the country, I'm not sure those four-inch-high stilettos make sense for getting around. Consider where you go and what styles work for getting you there. I once saw a mom pushing a stroller with twins in a suburban park. She was wearing a stunning leather coat and Jimmy Choos. She could barely chase after her toddlers, and when one stuck a lollipop to her fur collar, she lost it. I'm all for moms wanting to look sexy, but perhaps she should have saved it for a night on the town—not the sandbox.

If you've thought about all of this, then the ball is now in your court. How will you create your style? What will it communicate to the world about who you are? Years ago, I saw a woman at Galleries Lafayette in Paris who must have been in her seventies. She had a timeless beauty and an air of absolute elegance. But beyond that she had a fierce haircut and wore bright red lipstick and black eyeliner and a colorful scarf and clothes. I can't remark on one particular thing in detail, but the way she put herself together was so striking and confident that I could never forget her. She owned her style, and it left an indelible impression on me. We all need to find our own way to be that woman!

What is style?

Most people assume it's all about appearances: your clothes, your hair, your makeup. But I couldn't write a style chapter about owning it and allow you to go on thinking that way. Style is much more than what you see on the surface.

• It's the total package, a reflection of everything you have going on inside you: your thoughts, your dreams, your feelings, your attitude.

- It's how you express yourself: what you want to say and convey to the world.

- It's self-awareness and self-acceptance.

- It's your own unique spin, your individuality and creativity, which transform everything you touch.

- It's how you carry yourself: the way you walk, talk, and use your body language.

- It's the "essence" of who you are.

Try, try again

The best way to discover your style is to experiment. Think of it as an exercise in learning what works for you and what doesn't; you are training your style sense rather than shopping aimlessly. The key is to pay attention to what kinds of styles you are drawn to and why. And be open to anything and everything. Keep in mind:

- You don't have to shop in an expensive boutique or department store or max out your credit cards. You can find your style just as easily in a vintage store or a Target.

- No matter how something looks on a model or in a magazine, you need to feel like it looks good on you. I have learned that before I buy something, I have to love it and be able to envision myself wearing it multiple times in multiple situations. I have to feel totally comfortable in what I have on—the fit, the fabric, the color. Don't just buy something because it is in style or everyone else is wearing it.

- Dress for your body shape—don't try and hide behind your clothes. They should give you confidence and highlight your best assets rather than cover up what you perceive to be your flaws. I haven't always known what worked for my body. In fact I still have a healthy dose of body dysmorphia, as most of us do. But owning your style means being brave!

• Be honest. The most important aspect of finding your own style is being honest about how clothes make you look and feel. If you gaze in the mirror and don't 100 percent like what you see or the "vibe" it's giving you, then leave it behind. Anything I have been "iffy" about has wound up in the back of my closet for two years (and now in the Goodwill pile).

Mind Your Own Business: Do I need a style makeover?

In this day and age, reality TV shows are filled with people dropping hundreds of pounds and redoing their homes from floor to ceiling. So is it any wonder we're all makeover crazy? Over the years, I've had many clients come to me begging for a radical new look. I've learned there's always more to the story. No one just comes in on a whim and says "Dye my brown hair blond" or "Cut off ten inches." No one goes from soccer mom to sexpot without a damn good reason. There is something much more emotional that is usually driving it: a breakup, an affair, a wedding, a weight change, a new job. I'm fine with switching things up if you feel a new style will empower you. But do you *really* need a dramatic style change? Take this quiz and find out.

1. *The last time I weeded through my closet was:*

   A. yesterday.

   B. a decade ago.

   C. um . . . never.

2. *I would describe my style as:*

   A. cool and confident.

   B. dated and dour.

   C. a fashion emergency in the making.

3. *People tell me I remind them of:*

   A. Kate Middleton

   B. June Cleaver.

   C. Sid Vicious.

4. *My style makes me feel:*

   A. able to leap tall buildings in a single bound.

   B. able to go unnoticed at a singles bar.

   C. able to go to a Halloween party without a costume.

5. *For me, style is:*

   A. inner beauty reflected outward.

   B. a magazine that comes once a month in my mailbox.

   C. a waste of money.

   If you answered *mostly a's:* congratulations! Your style is working for you. It may need a few tweaks here and there, but no need to totally revamp (unless you have a good reason to do so).

If you answered *mostly b's*: you're living in a time warp. When was the last time you went shopping for something other than kitty litter? Your style needs to be refreshed. Start by sorting through your closet: what can stay and what has to go? Then supplement with small purchases to liven things up. No more being Miss Invisible . . .

If you answered *mostly c's*: unless you're planning a career in the circus or Gaga's entourage, it's time for a style do-over. Look, I started out with a punk style; I get the whole rebellion/artsy thing. The question to ask yourself is this: is my style holding me back? Is it conveying what I want people to know about me? Is it turning people on (as opposed to off)? If the answer is no or even maybe, you have my permission to press reboot.

CASE STUDY
The client who thought she needed a cut

As a hairdresser I am well aware that someone's external appearance can deeply influence how he or she feels on the inside. A great haircut can make someone walk a lot taller. Case in point: I had a client who asked me to cut off all of her hair. When I asked her why she wanted to make such an extreme change, she got quiet and revealed that she was coming out as a lesbian. I asked her why she thought coming out meant that she needed to have short hair, and she really wasn't sure. For her, she was identifying being gay with a specific style, and getting that style empowered her to be open about being that person. But only a few months later, happily dating a woman, my client came back to me and asked how we could get her hair to grow in faster. She missed her long hair and she realized that coming out didn't mean she couldn't keep her old style if she liked it.

Norma's Notes: BE TRUE TO YOU

My mother always told me not to be bullied into behaving like a sheep and following the trends. Dare to strike out! When I was a teenager, I was headed to see a punk band with my best friend. We were standing at a bus stop, and I was wearing a suit by a big Australian designer named Trent Nathan. The suit was very girly and straight out of the 1940s. But I had personalized it with a hot pink studded belt accented with several other studded belts— and I had written on my face in Japanese calligraphy. What can I say? This was my style at sixteen! A police car pulled up to the bus stop and the officers stepped out to arrest me because I was wearing a "lethal weapon." With no other choice, I surrendered my accessories to the cops and was left standing there in that girly suit without my belts. I definitely didn't feel so cool anymore. The next day, my mother marched down to the police station and demanded to get my personal property back. The police gave her the belts but warned her that they were considered dangerous. My mother thought the whole thing was utterly hilarious and ridiculous. She always encouraged me to embrace my own style and look different from the pack. And I always have.

Tabatha's Final Take: Own Your Style

* Style isn't just about fashion or beauty. It's also about the way you put yourself out there. The message you convey about who you are and who you want to be. It's not just what you wear, but how you wear it: your attitude, your confidence, your charisma.

* Owning your style is not being afraid to make it uniquely yours. Don't ever become a slave to the trends. Cookie-cutter is never chic.

* Your style should grow and evolve as you do. Don't let yourself become "stuck."

* Style is the one thing people never forget: think Jackie O, Audrey Hepburn, Madonna. Strive to be someone whose style leaves a lasting impression.

PART II

Own Your Business

4

Plan

. . . .

"Thanks to my father leaving us and seeing how my mother had left herself vulnerable because she trusted him, I made myself a promise. I would always be prepared, and I would always have a plan."

. . . .

M y father was an accountant by trade. He and my mother were partners in both business and life, and she trusted him not only because he was her husband but also because he was the money guy. Aside from the clubs, my parents ran an adult bookshop. (Hey, I never claimed to have a traditional childhood.) One day when I was about ten, my dad phoned my mom, who was at home with me. He asked her what was for dinner and told her to come pick him up at the store. So you can imagine how surprised my mother was when she arrived at the shop and it was closed with no sign of my father anywhere. He had left a suicide note, a five-dollar bill, and his wedding ring.

My mother was shocked, furious, and I think in some ways relieved. The next day, she went to the bank. Surprise again: my dad had been siphoning money out of their joint account for months and now there was nothing left. My father was a coward. I had always known that and so did my mom; he was too weak to say he wanted a divorce and, obviously, after taking all the money, he wasn't really planning on committing suicide. But it left my mom in a tough situation. We went from a very nice lifestyle to having nothing—and there was no one to shoulder the financial burden except her. She had to work four or five jobs just to pay the fees for my private school and keep our heads above water. Instantly our lives changed. Before my father left, she never went to the bank, she spent whatever she wanted, and she never had to manage the money. She let my father do it and without question. After he left, she had to be in charge of everything. So she learned how. Little by little, she pieced our lives back together and took the reins.

My father leaving us was a huge lesson for me, too: never let anyone be in charge of your life. It's your ass on the line, and there is no excuse (unless you're a child) to let anyone besides you make the plans. Going into business or frankly any relationship without understanding how things work and will work later (even if the shit hits the fan, like it did in my mother's case) is asinine. You might as well put on a blindfold or bury your head in the sand.

Unfortunately a lot of people are guilty of not being in charge and not having a plan. I can't tell you how many times I have walked into a struggling business and sat down with an owner who proudly declares, "I just decided to wing it!" Really? What a surprise! And you wonder why your business is a disaster and I'm here trying to save your ass? These people really piss me off! I start asking them questions about the basic financials of their business ("How much money is coming in vs. going out?" "What is your overhead?" "How much do you need to break even?") and their eyes become glassy. They look positively dumbfounded, as if I have just asked them to recite the encyclopedia. If you had a plan, you would know all these answers. If you *owned* that plan, you would not need me to fix the mess you made in the first place!

Case in point: I once worked with a salon owner who didn't have a business plan and was actually content to fly by the seat of her pants. She never balanced a checkbook, and she even allowed her clients to pay her in vodka instead of cash. This resulted in her utilities being cut off several times and her staff having to deal with nasty bill collectors looking for "the boss." The most infuriating thing to me was that she thought this "laid-back" behavior and lack of planning made her cool and hip. In the end it just made her broke, evicted, and out of business.

So let me be clear: no one can "just wing it." Anyone who claims they did and had success is lying. They are like those kids you went to school with who insisted they never studied for tests yet always managed to pull straight A's. I never believed them, and I'm convinced they were fibbing to impress me. Well, guess what? I am not impressed if you tell me you are "winging it" when it comes to your business. I think it's ridiculous and shows a lack of responsibility and commitment. You are being lazy and utterly unprepared. I don't care if you dread crunching numbers or putting thoughts to paper. If you want to run a business, you better get used to these things. And you better have a plan that you can stand behind with confidence and conviction.

The process of writing a business plan will . . .

- Help you ask the right questions so you don't miss anything. This will do a great deal to prevent you from screwing things up.

- Keep you grounded and remind you about what you're doing and why you're doing it—which comes in handy when you're freaking out and second-guessing yourself.

• Provide you with a road map. It shows the direction you want to be going in, where you want to wind up, and how you're going to get there.

• Reveal the capital you need to start your business and the cash flow needed to sustain it. It doesn't necessarily take a lot of money to make money, but it definitely will take some. You have to pay your own overheads, suppliers, and utilities before your customers start coming in and paying you.

• Keep you accountable and stop you from purchasing the pretty, shiny things instead of the practical ones that will help your business.

• Prove to anyone who is interested in helping you grow your business (such as a potential investor, a lending institute, or a friend/family member who is floating you some cash) that you have given this dream of yours a lot of thought and consideration. You're strategizing not just for today but also for the future.

Some people approach this task with as much enthusiasm as going for a root canal. It doesn't need to be that way. You don't have to be a financial whiz to write a good plan. I've seen some great plans come out of owners who can barely add 2+2 without a calculator! It can be as simple as breaking down what needs to go into realizing your vision, and creating clear action items on how to execute those steps.

I'm going to make it even easier for you (you can thank me later). I want you to answer the questions on page 48 to help you create each section of your plan. Don't just scribble something down. Give it serious thought. Then go back and edit and refine each part of your plan till it speaks to your vision.

Mind Your Own Business:
So, tell me about yourself

If you were face-to-face with someone and had to explain your business and who you are, what would you say . . . in three minutes or less? This exercise is a good way to summarize your intent in a concise, enthusiastic, and professional manner. I want you to act it out: actually pretend you are meeting a potential investor, or talking to a reporter. Or just visualize me, standing there in front of you. Take a deep breath, form your thoughts, and speak. Practice with a friend or in the mirror. Here's an example of something I'd like to hear:

Hello, my name is _____. I am opening a gluten-free bakery in _____ because there is a need in the community and no store filling it. My child has a gluten allergy, as do several of his schoolmates. As a mom, I know it is difficult to find products he can eat that are also healthy and taste great. I have had to bake them myself at home, since no store readily carries them. My breads, muffins, cakes, cookies, and pastries will be made fresh daily from the highest-quality ingredients. They will be delicious, and even people who do not have gluten allergies will love them!

Putting your plan together

Now that you have an idea of who you are, sell it to me. The first part of your plan is the **Mission Statement.** This should include who you are professionally, why you are capable of starting this business, and what you want to achieve, as well as what you need to get there. Eventually this will develop into your company description.

- Who am I, what do I do, and what do I bring to the table?

- What in my background (schooling, training, hands-on experience) makes me the perfect person to start this business?

- How do I see my business—what makes it special, unique, a necessary service in today's world?

- Who is my customer? What do they want/need that I—and no one else—can give them?

- What are my big-picture goals—where do I see the business going in the near and distant future?

- What do I need to do to achieve these goals (such as financial backing, an ideal location, a trained and dedicated staff, etc.)?

- Once I have the resources, what do I see happening? A booming business that fills a void in the local marketplace? A new, exciting service that will change the way people think or do things? Multiple locations around the country or the world?

Next comes your **Market Analysis.** This is an overview of the business sector you are entering. It pinpoints the competition and how you will differentiate yourself and be competitive. You will have to do a little digging to prove you can make it in the market.

I suggest starting with a search on the Internet and in the Yellow Pages. Maybe there are three other yogurt shops in your area and you had no idea. Maybe there is no hair salon that stays open on Sundays and you could be the only one. Try www.similarsites.com or calling your local chamber of commerce. Googletrends.com is a good site for getting a global picture of the market and proving that you are entering a sector that is projecting growth. For example, according to Google Trends, doughnut shops have showed a steady incline since 2011. Given that doughnuts are trendy, your doughnut business would be booming—especially when you bring your unique spin to it.

A visit to see how your competitors do things right/wrong is also in order. Put on your sleuthing cap and observe them in action. This isn't spying—it's obtaining necessary intelligence and market research. Social media (their Facebook page and Twitter account) are a great way to get to know the type of consumer you'll be dealing with. Check out reviews on Yelp, Yahoo, Zagat, Citysearch, Angie's List, MerchantCircle, Insider Pages, and other sites to see (straight from the customers' mouths) what they love/hate about the competition.

CASE STUDY
The owner with a half-ass plan

I worked with a salon where the owner had the unique idea to open a men-only salon. It was very smart in concept, and totally filled a void in the marketplace—so the guy had done his market research. The problem was his terrible business model. He wanted low prices, quick services, and high turnover (he thought all of these factors would bring in money faster). Instead, it created unsatisfied customers and a burned-out staff. I advised him to rethink it: quality service and slightly higher prices would be a better option. He couldn't do as many cuts, but he'd be building a loyal customer base and making his staff happier. I told him it's great to find a niche in the market, but you have to have the right plan behind it. If it's not working you need to be willing to change. Unfortunately, this owner wasn't. And I don't have to tell you what happened to his salon.

Finally, I recommend joining a trade association or attending conferences to learn the ins and outs of your particular business. You'll network and make great contacts that can help you down the road. You should always be looking ahead to how you can improve and evolve your product or service. Find out:

- How many similar businesses exist in the market I am entering?

- Are these businesses successful? Is there room in the market for another—or is there a need for someone to do it better? What are their strengths and weaknesses?

- Is there a need locally for this business (for example, there is no pizzeria in a forty-mile radius)?

- What is lacking in the market that I can satisfy? What do customers say they want/need?

- What will I do differently that will make my business stand out from the rest?

- What do suppliers think of my competition? Are they constantly reordering to meet a high demand?

The third piece of your plan is your company's **Structure and Staffing.** This will explain the organization and logistics of your business and how it functions. When you're writing this section of your plan, keep it as clear and concise as you can; it's easy to get lost in legalese. Explain how you see the business organized into one of the structures below. Different types of companies have different advantages when it comes to liability and taxes. If you're not sure which structure is best for you, check with the Small Business Association (www.sba.gov) or SCORE (Service Corps of Retired Executives) at www.score.org. Lawyers, financial advisers, and accountants can also give you some sound advice—but usually for a steep price. I always find investing in expertise worth the expense. Having a lawyer make sure you have done the paperwork correctly and give you advice that is outside of your wheelhouse can save you money in the long run.

SOLE PROPRIETOR: You own your company and are solely responsible for its assets and liabilities. The buck stops with you!

- Do I want to be my own boss?

- Am I okay handling all of the responsibilities of my business? Do I have the time and patience?

- Am I comfortable being financially responsible for my business—and do I have the money in the bank to do it?

PARTNERSHIP: You and another person share the responsibility—and profits/losses—of the business. It can be a fifty-fifty partnership, or one in which one person has more power/say.

- Am I a good team player?

- Do I want someone to help shoulder the burden of my new business?

- Do I want someone to split the costs up front?

- Will I be okay with giving as much as half of my profit to someone else?

- Will I be receptive to someone else's opinions when it comes to my business?

CASE STUDY
The partners who pissed each other off

I worked with a salon where the partners were at odds, and it was taking a toll on them and their staff. Their partnership didn't start off that way. In fact, all was fine for the first few years, but they never discussed the future. When you're in business with someone, you have to consider where the road might lead you. You have to put it on the table. These two never talked about how marriage and children would affect their partnership. What if one of them didn't want to be so involved in the day-to-day anymore? What if one of them wanted out?

So all of the above eventually came into play, and it created huge resentments. One partner felt she was shouldering all the burden, while the other felt that her priorities were different and she was not going to apologize for that. Partnership is truly a marriage, so you must plan the future together—all the what-ifs and possible scenarios. When you know what to expect of each other, you won't wind up at each other's throats. Life always changes, and partners have to be prepared.

CORPORATION: This is a larger, more complicated structure, with shareholders who own the business and are responsible for its actions and debts. To form a corporation you'll need to establish your business name and register it in your state. You may then need licenses and permits to operate. Complicated? Yes. But the good news is that shareholders' personal assets are protected, even if your business goes belly-up. The corporation is a separate entity from the people who founded it. The larger you grow, the greater the risk to your personal assets and the more you may need to protect them.

- Do I see my business as a larger venture—one that requires a large structure to oversee it?
- Do I plan to own the company by myself—or will I bring in investors?
- Do I see this as a possible franchise?
- Am I okay with other people having a say in my business?

LLC (LIMITED LIABILITY COMPANY): It has the limited liability of a corporation and the tax advantages of a partnership. In the eyes of the government, an LLC is not a separate tax entity. The owners are technically "members." Depending on the state, you can be the sole member. A lawyer will have to set one up for you and can explain the pros and cons.

- Do I worry what will happen to my personal finances if my business flops?

- Am I concerned about lawsuits or debts arising from my business?

- Am I someone who prefers not to take big risks?

- Will I sleep better knowing I have limited liability?

Once you know how you want your business structured, you need to decide on who will do the work. When I opened my salon, I knew that staff would be one of the most important components. I wanted well-trained, motivated hairdressers who wanted to build a future and were invested in their careers. I also wanted a manager, as that would help me be an effective owner. I was happy to start slowly, so my first staff consisted of only seven people: myself, three stylists, a manager, and two assistants. Consider how many people you need to effectively get things off the ground. Your team can grow as your business does.

- How many employees will I hire?

- What will their specific jobs be, and how many hours a day/week will they put in?

- How much will I pay them and what other compensation am I offering?

- What will be my total cost of staff per week/month/year?

• Am I offering training, education?

Part four is the **Marketing and Sales Strategies.** Once you have a business, you need to spread the word to your target audience. This step further defines who that audience is and how you will reach them.

• How are my competitors branding and promoting themselves? How can I do it better?

• Who is my key audience—and what message do I want to convey to them about my business? What is a short and sweet slogan that tells what I am all about?

• In what ways will I promote my business? Will I create a Web site and use e-mail blasts, Facebook, Twitter, print ads, mailings, etc.? What will be the most effective means of reaching a large audience? What will be the most cost efficient?

• In what ways can I publicize my business? Consider local media that might cover it, trade organizations that might support it, referrals and contacts who are willing to spread the word. Now is the time to call in all your chips!

CASE STUDY
The cupcaker who went door-to-door

This story is actually about a family member of mine—my brother's wife to be exact. When their daughter was diagnosed with severe diabetes, my sister-in-law knew she wanted to be able to stay home with her daughter and give her the care she needed. She decided to give up her job, so she came up with an idea for a home-based baking business. She knew how popular cupcakes were, and she decided that they would be her focus. Now most small businesses that start in someone's kitchen don't usually take off like this. But my sister-in-law launched a serious marketing campaign. She went to every store, café, and restaurant in Melbourne, Australia, gave samples, and introduced them to her cupcakes. She told all her friends that if they knew anyone having a party or event to call her. She also spent every weekend at farmers' markets and local events spreading the word. Amazingly, her phone started ringing and her business is now booming. It goes to show that you don't always need money to promote yourself. Sometimes all you need is a little ingenuity, a good product, and some good old-fashioned pounding the pavement.

The last part of your plan is probably the most important (and the one that scares people the most!). It's your **Financial Projections**. You're going to need to show this to any investor—a bank loan officer, a venture capitalist, or even your dad—who is lending you some cash. They want to see real numbers. How fast is your business going to grow and turn a profit? How quickly can you repay them?

Remember that these projections are not written in stone, and no one is going to slap your wrist for being optimistic. It's you hedging your bets and hoping for the best—which is all you can do at this point in this unpredictable marketplace. I urge you to be realistic and not overinflate your projections. Investors won't believe your barrette and hair ribbon business is going to earn a billion dollars in five years! There has to be reasoning/credible sourcing behind your forecast. If you do your homework, you should have no problem backing up your plan with adequate sourcing. Both the National Federation of Independent Business (www.nfib.com) and the Small Business Administration (www.sba.gov) can help you with templates and local assistance.

Start with a financial forecast.

It's like looking into a crystal ball and guesstimating (based on the market, your experience, and how much your competitors make) how much money you will earn over the next three to five years.

Calculate an expense budget.

Really consider how much financing you will need, keeping in mind that cash flow is critical to the survival of any business. Go back over your previous business plan sections—this will help you anticipate where the costs lie.

How much will I need to get my business off the ground? What are the start-up costs?

How much will I need to pay employees?

How much will I need to spend on promotion/marketing?

What kind of a reserve of cash will I need if the business has an off month? You don't want a down cycle to close your doors.

Are there any variable costs? (For example, you're a florist and certain flowers are more expensive when they are out of season.)

Do I need to pay for initial permits/licenses/equipment?

Estimate how much you will need to borrow.

This debt will figure heavily into your profitability.

What are my monthly loan payments?

What is the interest I have to pay monthly/yearly?

How long will it take me to pay back the loan in its entirety?

Develop a cash-flow chart.

A simple spreadsheet can help you chart how money will flow into and out of your business on a weekly, monthly, and yearly rate. It will also show you the bottom line: how much you could take in after all your expenses.

In a good month, how much can I anticipate making?

With optimal growth, what could my business turn in a year?

With optimal growth, what could my business turn in three years?

Norma's Notes: ALWAYS HAVE A PLAN B

I didn't see my father again until I was twenty-one, and it was a brief, chance encounter. Once my mother got on her feet, we moved to start a new life. Although she didn't have a Plan B

(nobody expects her husband to disappear and take all the money with him), she didn't throw in the towel. Norma said there are two choices when things go wrong: "Stay down or get up." She chose to get up.

You can't always plan for the unexpected, but you need to be flexible, to think on your feet, and to not give up. When I owned my first salon, I was faced with four pipes that burst one very cold December morning. The place was flooding, and I needed to think fast and hatch a new plan. I called a local competitor and explained what had happened, and asked if they had any room for my staff to work. Their space was small, but they were kind and managed to accommodate some of us—so I could take care of my customers who couldn't wait. It took two days for the water to be pumped out, the pipes to be fixed, and everything to be cleaned up, but I covered my ass.

Tabatha's Final Take: Own Your Plan

✳ Your business plan is a way for you to think through and organize how your business will be built and operate.

✳ Make sure your plan includes goals that indicate where you want to be in the future. A business cannot remain flat. There has to be a plan for growth and targets you want to hit.

✳ This is not a doctoral thesis. Keep it simple and to the point. But don't mistake simple with simpleminded. You need to think through every aspect of the business and ask every question so that you can pick and choose what is important to include in your plan. And remember, the person reading your plan isn't as familiar with it as you are, so you need to make your ideas clear.

✳ Always proofread your work. This document needs to look good as well as contain great ideas. Make sure you present a polished plan.

✳ What can you add to your plan that really brings the business to life? Can you offer photographs of a proposed location or the design sketches? A sample product? Mock-ups of your logo? All of these items bring the business off the page and make it real for the reader.

✳ Make sure that you know the answers to any and all questions you may be asked. You should know your business inside and out.

5

Money

"I still remember my first paycheck. I worked in my parents' club doing the lights. I was so excited. I had always been given money to do chores around the house, but it was five bucks here and ten bucks there. My first paycheck (about a hundred dollars), especially when I was ten years old, felt like a million bucks."

As much as I enjoy shopping for a hot new pair of Louboutins, I have always been a saver. As a kid, it gave me a sense of security and self-worth. I had two favorite ways to stash my cash: a Christmas club (you put in a few dollars weekly and it accumulated in time for Christmas shopping) and layaway plans. It might have taken me months to pay off that hot new outfit, but it was worth it. What thrilled me was the sense of waiting for what I really wanted, saving up for it, then paying it off in full. It made me appreciate it even more when I finally got it.

The staggering personal debt that the average American has on credit cards is amazing. Almost no one saves anymore. Even more shocking to me is how many business owners completely miss the concept of saving. They see money coming in and they think they can use the till like an ATM. For them, it's cash in . . . cash out. I'm happy to hear that your customers are paying you, but that doesn't give you permission to waste everything you've earned. There is a big difference between cash flow and profit.

Part of owning your money is learning to be responsible with it. I don't care how much that new "It Bag" is calling to you. If you don't have enough money in the bank to cover your necessary costs for the next few months, forget about it. I worked with a salon owner in California who was a shopaholic. Her staff knew all about it because she would ditch out of work to go to the mall. And her customers knew all about it because she would put on fashion shows for them. Only her husband had no idea. While he was robbing Peter to pay Paul and canceling his health insurance to pay the salon's rent, his wife was spending what she made behind the chair. It was a horrible situation: they had two small children! Yet every day, the boss showed up in a new outfit. It was a challenge showing her that you can't always have what you want when you want it. I advised her to come clean—to admit she had spent herself into a corner and she needed to take responsibility for it. She had caused these problems, and she needed to be honest about it. When she did, people were understanding and supportive. With a little help from her friends, she got back on track. And now I am happy to say her bills are paid, her salon is doing well, and her husband can afford insurance.

On the other end of the spectrum is someone who actually does make enough to cover expenditures but is foolish with how much he spends and what he spends it on. One salon owner I worked with in New Jersey prided himself on being flashy (that's putting it mildly) and loved to act like a big shot, throwing his money around. He spent lots of dough on lavish cars, parties, and clothes, and as a function of his needing to make more and more money, his business began to suffer. "Why are you doing this?" I asked him. It seemed ridiculously irresponsible. Then I got to the root of the problem: he was squandering his money because he thought owning all these fancy things would make people like him and make his staff respect him. Well, a champagne fountain is not a reason to like or respect someone. In fact, his staff wound up respecting him a lot more when he took ownership of his finances and acted more responsibly.

It wasn't easy to get through to him, though. I had to make him literally throw money out the window to show him that this was *exactly* what he was doing. I told him, "If you want respect, you need to earn it," and that it started with him respecting his money. In the end, he took my advice to heart. Instead of blowing money on expensive champagne, he put it back into the business. And now he's opened a second location and almost all of his staff is still with him.

CENTS AND SENSIBILITY

As a business owner, how much you sock into savings will depend on how your business is doing, your financial plan, and your hopes for the future. Always keep the big picture in mind. What are you saving up money for? Ideally not to buy yourself more clothes or throw parties. You should sock away savings . . .

- so you can pay off your debt more quickly.
- to build a cushion for a slow time of year or something breaks.
- to invest in further educating yourself and your staff.
- to pay for advertising to reach a broader customer base.
- to hire a new staff, upgrade equipment, expand your current business, or add another location.

Smart money

Being responsible with your money—truly owning it—means making wise decisions. Sometimes it's as simple as: "Do I really need that pink leopard, faux-fur coat?" (I can practically guarantee the answer is NO!) Other times, it's paying your credit card bill in full (instead of the minimum) so you don't rack up interest fees. Remember when you were a kid and you wanted something and your parents told you that you had to wait? You probably hated them for it. Well, being a business owner is like that. It's knowing when to say yes, when to say no, and when to say later. It's also being honest and realistic about your finances and what you can and can't afford. It isn't always fun: it sucks when you have to watch your pennies and can't afford to go on vacation or buy those TVs that would be so great in the waiting area. It's hard admitting to yourself and others that you aren't flush with funds. You're not the only one in that situation—people just love to live beyond their means and embellish how well they are doing to make them feel valid. I would prefer to Own It and know that forfeiting those TVs or that vacation gets me one step closer to financial success, freedom, and retiring in style.

The first step is determining when and where you *really* need to spend and when you don't. Maybe there is something essential that your business is lacking. I want you to really challenge yourself before you reach for the checkbook or credit card. Ask yourself, "Can my business be successful without it and for how long?" But other times, you may need to spend money on yourself. You have been working for two years straight and you are burned-out. Instead of trying to justify "splurging" on a Hawaiian resort you can't afford, try a staycation exploring your own city. It's all about balance and making the right choices. Yes, you need a car to get around—but do you really need a Porsche? Part of being a grown-up is putting your finances where they can best serve you—not acting like a kid in a candy store.

Mind Your Own Business: Am I a saver ... or a spender?

Before you can work on owning your money, you need to understand what your financial style is. Take this quiz and answer the questions honestly.

1. *In my wallet, I have ...*

   A. so many credit cards I can't keep track.

   B. ten dollars cash till my next paycheck.

   C. a credit card for emergencies and enough cash to get me through the day.

2. *I see a big SALE sign in a department store window. I ...*

   A. run in before someone beats me to it!

   B. ask if I can open a store credit account and purchase a whole fall wardrobe for an additional 15 percent off.

   C. keep on walkin'. That sign's probably always in the window trying to woo customers in.

3. *My boss gives me a bonus check for my hard work on a project. I ...*

   A. immediately book a vacation to Hawaii.

   B. have it already spent—I am behind on my rent and credit card payments.

   C. sock it away in a CD where I can't touch it for at least a year.

4. *My great-aunt dies and leaves me an inheritance. I will . . .*

   A. make sure I spend it on things I really need (like a new sports car . . . a cool leather jacket . . . a party for my friends).

   B. use it to pay back the money I owe my parents (so they'll let me borrow again!).

   C. invest it wisely with a financial adviser's help, so it makes me more money in the future.

5. *If I won the lottery, I would . . .*

   A. live like a millionaire!

   B. live without fear of debt collectors stalking me.

   C. live like I do now. That money will be my nest egg for retirement.

If you answered *mostly a's*: you need to cut up your credit cards and sit on your hands. No more shelling out money on a whim. May I direct you to Shopaholics Anonymous?

If you answered *mostly b's*: you are in over your head. Do you like drowning in debt? No? Then do something about it. Make a financial plan to dig yourself out, little by little, then don't let it happen again. This isn't Monopoly money . . . it's your future.

If you answered *mostly c's*: you and Scrooge might be mates. I appreciate that you prefer to put your money away rather than squandering it. But I would also give yourself permission now and then to splurge a little. You've earned it.

By the books

Most people treat bookkeeping and accounting as a necessary evil or ignore it altogether. I like keeping track of my money because it makes me feel in control. I don't care how you keep track of your budget—in a notebook or on a computer—but do it. I know it's time-consuming. I am not an accountant, so especially in the beginning, when I owned my first salon, I knew I needed an expert to make sure the job was done properly and someone who could teach me what was a tax deduction and what wasn't. Seek out an accountant who is an expert in your field of business; he or she will know the specifics better than anyone. Accountants aren't "one size fits all." Case in point: I once submitted a receipt to my accountant for a pricey dinner. He questioned the amount; it seemed a bit extravagant for a dinner. I explained that it wasn't just me filling my face. It was a wrap party for my entire team and a necessary expense (and therefore a deduction) for the season of work I put in. He scratched his head: "What's a wrap party?" Clearly, he wasn't the guy for me!

The goal of any business is to do well and make a profit, and when you do, that's the time to start thinking long term and investing money. When I got to that point, I decided I needed someone to guide me. But the "financial adviser" I met with reminded me too much of a used-car salesman. He was pushy . . . and he was a little slippery. I assured him that I was no different from anyone else: I want my money to work hard for me, and I would like to retire one day and not worry. He assured me he could help me set things up for the future. Yet the meeting left me feeling uneasy, and I didn't like being told what I had to do with my money without a conversation (big surprise!). I also didn't feel comfortable with my money being tied up and untouchable in accounts and investments. What if I had an emergency and needed it? I felt like I was relinquishing control of my life, not just my finances. So I took my money elsewhere because this wasn't the right person for me.

I am not for a second implying that all financial advisers work this way nor would I discourage you from hiring one. I just think it comes down to what you are comfortable with. I learned that I need to be informed and then make my own choices for investing in my retirement while still having options for my future business endeavors.

FINDING THE RIGHT NUMBERS PERSON

There are many reasons owners hire financial advisers and accountants. I spoke of mine: I wanted an expert to set me up with a good system of checks and balances, and I wanted an adviser to help me grow my money and plan for the long term. You may have a much simpler reason: you are not good with figures, so you want someone to track them for you. Consider the size of your business. If it's small, you don't need an entire accounting firm. A bookkeeper or accountant might suffice. This person or this group will likely do several things for you, depending on how much you want to delegate. They can handle payroll, pay bills, prepare taxes, and offer you sound financial advice.

But here is my word of warning: make sure you are not signing away your money to someone. You want someone who communicates well so you always feel in control and understand the math. You may think it's great having someone take the reins for you, but we have all heard stories about people who have been burned and left with nothing because they weren't taking an active role in their finances. It helps to have a referral and always check references. You wouldn't hire babysitters for your kid without checking up on them first. This person is going to be "babysitting" your money!

Stupid money mistakes business owners make

Some very smart people make some very stupid mistakes with their finances. I can't tell you why. If I could knock some sense into them, I would. I assume it is a reaction to their situation. The worst mistakes usually spring from desperation, as in "I can't pay my bills, so I'll just sign up for another credit card." What I can tell you is that we are all guilty of making poor financial decisions now and then. According to the Small Business Administration, 33 percent of new small businesses fail within the first two years, and 56 percent fail within the first four years. Why? Because they probably didn't avoid the most common money mishaps:

- Draining your savings and your nest egg. I get it: you want to give your all to your business. That doesn't mean all your money. It's shortsighted to deplete all your savings to get things off the ground. What if the business fails? What if it takes longer than anticipated to turn a profit? What are you supposed to live on when your business isn't supporting you?

- Not saving for a rainy day. Shit happens. Your roof might leak; the basement might flood; a competitor might move in down the block and steal all your customers. Are you prepared for an emergency? You should always have at least three to six months of your expenses in a rainy-day fund. You never know, and you'll sleep better at night if you're prepared.

- Ignoring your retirement. You're not always going to be this gung ho to work. One day, I promise you, you'll be tired and you'll want to hang up your hat. Guess what? If you have no retirement savings, you won't be able to comfortably. Putting just a little away every paycheck is all it takes.

• Using one credit card to pay off another. Do you think this is getting you any further out of debt? All it's telling you is that you have spent like a drunken sailor. And it's not reducing what you owe; it's probably just getting angry bill collectors temporarily off your back (the new ones will be on your case soon enough!).

• Lending money when you don't have it (to employees, family members, friends, etc.). Are you a bank? Being generous is a lovely gesture, but not at the expense of your own financial well-being.

• Not comparing prices. Shop around for products and equipment—chances are you'll find what you're looking for somewhere cheaper. Be lazy and you'll pay more, for sure.

• Not paying bills on time. "I forgot" is not an excuse. You'll rack up late fees and higher interest if you don't stay on top of due dates. Do you have a calendar? Use it.

• Allowing someone else to be in charge. This goes back to my encounter with that first accountant who wanted to tell me what to do with my money. Letting someone else call the shots is a recipe for disaster (and how a lot of owners get ripped off by their employees). You need to know how much money you have and where it's going and when. An owner should always be in the know. Even if you hate dealing with dollar signs, don't delegate that job to someone else.

• Tossing your receipts. One of the biggest things I needed to learn as an owner was to keep and track receipts. I wasn't great at it; they were annoying little pieces of paper that I would either decline or eventually toss out. I thought of them as clutter (and I detest clutter!). When my accountant sat me down and explained how important those little pieces of paper were (they prove how much you spent come tax time and they make it easy to see where your money is going), it was a life-changing moment. I am now the queen of receipts, and my accountant (who bills by the hour) has to spend a lot less time figuring out my finances. I suggest getting yourself an accordion folder and filing receipts under categories (transportation, meals, supplies/equipment, promotions/marketing, etc.). You can also purchase software and a scanner and keep track of them on your computer in a spreadsheet. Another great tip: get a corporate credit card. That way all expenses you put on it are for your business (and you just need to keep the monthly statement).

Fixing a money mess

There is nothing more stressful than bills piling up and debt collectors stalking you. I've met people who ducked for cover every time the phone rang! If you have fallen behind in payments or racked up too much debt, don't avoid the issue (as I have found many owners do). Hoping it will go away is not the answer. It won't. You know what I am going to tell you: Own It! If you are having trouble making payments, pick up the phone, explain the situation, and work out a solution. It may take months; it may take years. It won't happen overnight unless you suddenly win the lottery. Once you pay down the debt, you'll need to make sure your credit report reflects it. Finally, make sure this doesn't happen again. What can you do to ensure you stick to a budget? How can you guarantee you won't miss another payment? (How about setting up an automatic online payment through your bank?) Are there expenses you can eliminate to reduce your monthly payout?

CASE STUDY
The partner who was
a financial F-up

The first question you need to ask before you agree to partner with someone in business is: do I trust them with the financials? If you have doubts about their financial solvency, decision making, or ethics then don't do it! This issue is way too important not to be 100 percent sure. I worked with a salon where the owners were friends and decided to go into business together. Just one big problem: one was financially secure and had assets; the other one had filed for bankruptcy and had nothing she could bring to the table financially. Needless to say by the time I got there, things were bad. One owner had all the debt in her name and hadn't taken a paycheck for months; meanwhile her partner took her money out daily, loved buying things that the salon didn't need and couldn't afford, and wasn't feeling any of the financial burden. Why should she? Her name wasn't on anything! She could continue with her horrible spending habits because her business partner allowed her to. I was amazed that these women were in business together—they couldn't have been more opposite. One was financially responsible and balanced her checkbook down to the penny, while the other was a reckless spender who had racked up so much debt it made my head spin. When I asked the responsible owner, "Why would you go into business with someone who was bankrupt and therefore clearly not good with money?" she shrugged. "She's my friend," she told me. "I thought she would change." Well, think again! Before you go into business with anyone, make sure you are financially on the same page. One of you can't be spending while the other is footing the bill.

Norma's Notes: A "ME" SPREE

My mother always told me if you have to ask someone how much it costs, then you can't afford it. And if you can't afford something, then you can't enjoy it. I always keep this in mind. There are certain times when I reward myself, and that's okay. If it's a birthday, a big career move, or a time when I have been working my ass off and deserve a little something, I'll go shopping. I buy what I can afford, what I feel is an investment, and what I will love and use. I shop for myself; I don't need to impress anyone. We have all met the people who need to show off or brag about what they have and how much it cost. I find that gauche. When I buy something it's for my own pleasure, not to rub in someone's face. And shouldn't that always be the case?

Tabatha's Final Take: Own Your Money

Most people don't like to discuss money—it's a taboo topic. But if you own it, you're not afraid anymore. You're secure in your savings and comfortable in your spending.

❋ Practice discipline. Save up for the things you need and don't buy anything unless you can afford it now. The best things in life are worth waiting for.

❋ Keep track of your spending. Write down every penny you earn and spend, and file receipts (you'll need them for taxes).

❋ Save for a rainy day. Every business owner needs an emergency fund. Hopefully you'll never need to use it. But if you do, isn't it nice to know it's there?

❋ Fess up to your financial screwups. If you've overspent or underbudgeted, come clean. Get yourself back on track by forging a plan. Negotiate with your lenders by being honest instead of hiding. Honesty is what earns you respect.

6

Brand

. . . .

*"I realized early in my career that I was a brand—even though at
the time I wasn't quite sure what 'Tabatha Coffey' meant. I had
built a steady clientele that was driven by word of mouth and
referrals. My customers had latched on to me, and I was distin-
guishing myself from other people in my line of work."*

. . . .

Hi, I'm Tabatha. I'm a hairdresser from London, and I'd
like to give you a service for free. If you like it, come back
and tell your friends to come in!" When I first arrived in
the United States as a young hairdresser, this was my line. And I
used it on every person I could get to listen to me at the mall, at the
M·A·C store, on the street. I still had my London punk aesthetic,
complete with a shaved head, and I tried to own it with my spiel.
Some people ran in fear of my "foreign" looks, some people ignored
me and walked away, but some were intrigued enough to come in
and try the "exotic" new hairdresser.

Slowly and surely, I built up my core clientele. Within a year, I
had a real business with a loyal following. And for the first time, I
really thought about my brand. I was a professional and needed to
adapt to the area and clientele I had coming in, but I still needed to
be true to myself. I didn't want to look like everyone else, and that

was okay. But I did need to modify a few things to make my brand appealing to the demographic I needed to reach. What my loyal clients loved about me (my honesty and edgy look) intimidated other people. So I had to temper it and adapt. I had to strike a balance.

Most small-business owners don't think about branding themselves. They assume only big corporations—the Walmarts, the Nikes, the Starbucks of the world—are brand worthy. Not true! If you have a business, you have a brand—even without the swanky logo. The big questions: Is it the brand you want or not? Do your vision and your brand have synergy?

Your brand should set you apart from your competitors and represent the values and personality of your product or service. It can symbolize passion, fun, confidence, trust, a set of values, or a combination of them. Essentially it should represent the experience your customer will have and what you want their perception of you to be. It is what you do and how you do it. Ultimately, building your brand is building your business's reputation. If you have a strong brand then you should know what someone will think or say when they hear the name of your business.

A good brand allows you to have a clear message, which tells customers who you are and why they should choose you. But the emotional attachment to your brand or the experience it creates is what will keep customers coming back and telling their friends about you.

··

THE BENEFITS OF BRANDING

So why go through all this trouble?

* Branding is a great way to get you noticed.
* People will have an easier time remembering you and your business.
* You can extend your brand to include new products and services you never even considered before.
* Having a strong focus will help overall effectiveness.
* Clarity and consistency create a sense of confidence with customers.

··

Before you can Own Your Brand, you need to first understand what a brand is and what it isn't. Many business owners make the mistake of thinking that all they need to do is get a logo. Logos are definitely part of a brand, but a brand is really all about giving your business a clear identity and personality. A brand is much, much more than a logo. A strong brand represents your vision, mission statement, staff, customers, product, service, surroundings, and strategy.

A brand is . . .

* Who you are, who you want to be, and who people perceive you to be. In my case, it's "honest, empowering, and caring." Start out trying to identify three pillars you want associated with your business and build around those.

* Your promise to your customer. What they can expect from your products and services. Again, identify the most important attribute your product or service can have and build on that.

• The thing that differentiates your business from your competitors'. Communicate this difference as a positive aspect of your business and not a negative about someone else's.

A brand is not . . .

• A bunch of words or slogans that are empty and lack follow-through. You must back up your claims with the real work. Empty claims will lead to disappointment and failure.

• Something you make up as you go along. A brand needs to be planned and carefully built. Once you put something out in the world, it's hard to take it back. So have a plan.

• Just one thing like a cute logo or a radio jingle. A brand is a strategy that encompasses all aspects of your business's personality and needs to be consistent. Don't say one thing on the radio and another thing a week later in print.

• Defined by anyone but you. Your customers don't determine your brand identity. You do. If you have a bad Yelp review or an unhappy customer, you need to fix that. You need to take charge of the perception of your business.

Mind Your Own Business:
Give your brand a face

Here's a little game to get you thinking. I like to tell owners to think of their brand as a person or a personality.

It's a creative way to brainstorm and help you "put a face" on what you are trying to convey. Close your eyes and consider . . .

* What does this person act like, dress like, sound like?
* What makes them stand out?
* Are they fun, serious, silly, funny, educated?
* Are they sophisticated, youthful, mature?
* Who will like them? Why are they likable?
* What do they stand for and believe in?
* How do they conduct themselves?
* What are they skilled at?
* What do they represent?
* What color would better suit this person?
* What symbols or letters would best represent them?
* What name would a person like this have?
* What words would you use to describe this person?
* What catchphrase or sentence would tell another person how to describe them?
* What would tell people all they need to know about this person?

When you own your brand, you don't just pass out business cards. You also eat, sleep, and breathe its philosophy. You are a walking, talking example of your brand in action. You may feel like that's a whole lot of pressure—and it is! Imagine if I woke up for a speaking engagement and decided not to bother styling my hair. What would people say about the pride I take in my work, in my appearance, and in my brand?

Dolly Parton once told a late-night host that she gets dolled up even to do the grocery shopping. When he asked why, she said that her fans had come to expect nothing less of her, and she would never disappoint them. And who doesn't love Dolly and know exactly who she is? She has built one of the most iconic brands in music.

Branding doesn't apply just to celebrities. Every business owner needs to remember that he/she as well as his/her staff are the ambassadors of the brand. This is the whole theory behind uniforms. A uniform is a clear way to define and communicate a brand. But what do you think when you get to the register at a McDonald's and the person taking your order has a dirty uniform? The details matter, and part of owning your brand is paying attention to every detail. I have heard employees complain that their boss is stingy about paying for additional or replacement uniforms. This is very shortsighted. If you leave your employee with no choice but to wear something that is soiled or worn out, then you are damaging your own brand.

CASE STUDY
The genius that is Mickey D's!

Sometimes two nearly identical products are miles apart in terms of their public perception. One might be regarded as better, cooler, safer, more upmarket, or more reliable. Why? Branding! And sometimes branding can be so powerful that it actually sways your behavior.

One of my favorite brands is McDonald's, but not for the

reasons you might think (namely Big Macs and fries!). When I am at home in the United States, I rarely if ever eat at a McDonald's. But I travel overseas a lot for work, and there always comes a point when I am tired, lonely, and homesick. Because of the incredibly strong branding, I know I can go to any McDonald's in the world and order a meal without having to speak the language and it will taste relatively the same as it would in the United States. The restaurants look the same as the ones in New York or L.A. Even the packaging is identical. In those situations, McDonald's represents comfort, consistency, and home to me, which is why I go in and order a meal. McDonald's has built a brand that represents this to a lot of people, which is why they have achieved global success. This kind of brand equity is what makes us depend on certain companies over others.

Building your brand

If you're not a fast-food chain, the process of branding may scare the crap out of you. It sounds like a mammoth task . . . but it's not. A brand evolves, but it is not something you can just change on a whim; it needs to be strategically built. As I own my brand, I think long and hard about what I stand for and how to communicate it clearly. Sometimes the message can shift, but the pillars are always the same. If you come up with a strong foundation for your brand, you will be on your way to owning it.

I like to break it down into five easy steps:

1. What are you trying to say?

What does your brand stand for? What promises or claims is it going to make? Make sure it's attainable! Don't promise that your product will help people grow hair unless it does. Some bald guy is going to call you out on it! You should always be able to deliver on the messaging and communicate it clearly. Be specific. It isn't enough to just say "We stand for quality." Frankly, that could mean anything. What is your brand going to do to stand out from the crowd?

That said, KISS (keep it simple, stupid). The name of your brand should not be tough to spell or pronounce or be too complex. You want people to remember it and be able to ask for it—think of Apple, Coke, or Amazon. It doesn't have to be dull. Extra points if you're evocative and clever. Just make certain it broadcasts the message you want to convey. And don't be too clever because, like a vanity license plate, it can be a turnoff if it is trying too hard to be clever or smart and requires work from the customer to make sense of it.

2. Who are you trying to attract?

You need to decide who your core audience will be. It's easy for owners to say, "I want everyone." But let's face it: that isn't going to happen. What age group is your business best suited for? What income level is more likely to spend money with you? Is your business gender specific?

3. Be consistent.

Any good brand is consistent so as not to confuse customers. There must be a clear accuracy in how everything is presented, from the name of your business and the colors you use, to the way employees speak and act, how and where you market, and the social media you use. If you define your brand as geared toward women, don't choose masculine colors or language for your pamphlets or Web site. Right off the bat, you would be having a brand identity crisis!

4. Be confident.

Once you have established what your brand is and what it stands for, you need to stand behind it, beside it, and in front of it 100 percent. You need to believe in it and be able to sell it to everyone in a loud, strong, and confident voice. If you don't believe in your brand, who else will?

5. Don't give up.

Just like building a business takes time, so does creating a brand. Just because you put it out there, it may not stick right away. Keep at it. You need to continue to build your pillars of your brand and try to amplify its reach.

BRANDS THAT BLOW MY MIND

I want you to think about some of your favorite brands and how you perceive them. Why do they resonate for you? Look at them as case studies and try to apply what they do well to your business. Here are three of my faves.

- **APPLE** is an amazing brand because it has intense clarity and simplicity. It is one of the only companies that has been able to repackage the same product and sell it over and over again to a loyal clientele. Let's face it: we don't all need an iPad and an iPad mini, and an iPhone and an iPod. But many of us have all of these in our technology arsenal. Why? Because we believe Apple when they say these things are necessary and desirable to our everyday life. Brilliant branding and marketing!

- **TARGET** is another great brand. It is a big-box store that has managed to create a coherent brand around a wide diversity of lower-price-point products. The idea of bringing in high-end designers such as Phillip Lim, Peter Pilotto, Anna Sui, Zac Posen, and Jean Paul Gaultier to do lower-price-point lines has changed the retail business. They made big-box shopping sexy and cool to upmarket customers. Just think of how many people wait in line every time a chic new designer unveils a Target line. It's the promise of owning a couture look for about twenty dollars, and who can say no to that?

- **MADONNA** is the most successful example of celebrity branding I can think of. Madge has changed her style, look, music, and persona more times than any music artist. From *Like a Virgin* to *Erotica* to *Ray of Light* and everything she has done in between, Madonna has evolved her style while still building her unique brand. Her brand is about being a work in progress while remaining true to her beliefs. She stands for strong, sexy, powerful. She is one of the few artists who continues to be relevant thirty years after her career began.

Spread the word

In this day and age, social media and the Internet are two of the best ways to get your brand out to the masses. Keep the message consistent across all platforms. This helps bring recognition and awareness. You can't run one logo on Facebook and another on your Web site. Make sure that all info is current and up-to-date. Social media only work when you keep them relevant and fresh. Remember that (thanks to Google!) a Web site is often the first impression a customer may have of your product. It is amazing how many businesses don't want to invest the time or money in a site that is a good representation of their brands. If your site is dated, not user-friendly, and cheap or amateur-looking, that is the perception a potential client will have of your brand and business.

Conversely, remember that all of your customers have access to their own social media, as well as user-generated content review sites like Yelp. Customers have a lot of power to spread the word about your brand. It's critical to keep your customers happy so that people on Twitter and out in the blogosphere sing your praises. And when you do receive a negative review, it's equally important to remedy the problem if it is legitimate and manage the fallout from that public forum.

Some businesses may see a benefit from hiring a publicist or PR consultant. This can be helpful if you need to manage professional media, such as magazine or TV interviews, or even engage in professional or public speaking. But this can be a costly expense (as much as $5,000+ a month!), so I suggest you try to manage your brand yourself wherever and whenever possible.

Brand today, gone tomorrow

Sometimes, we have to make some branding mistakes to discover what our customers really value about our business. Corporate businesses often talk about "rebranding" as a strategy to grow their customer base. But the trick is to not alienate the loyal customers you already have. This is a delicate proposition because in order to entice someone new, you may have to change the very thing that a current customer loves. So I caution you: don't rebrand too quickly. If you decide your brand is not working, keep in mind that it is a major undertaking to change it completely, and you will need a strong plan. Sometimes rebranding works; sometimes it doesn't.

Case in point: in 2010 when the Gap tried to launch a new logo, customers rebelled. A new logo is a gamble. The goal is to freshen or update a brand while continuing to message its core values. That is challenging, and in the case of the Gap it didn't work. It wasn't that customers didn't like the new design (a small blue box over the *P*). They felt it didn't stand for anything—namely how the Gap planned to change. The company's president said it was a more "contemporary" logo, but it was an empty one in terms of reflecting anything significant about the brand's core values.

Similarly, JCP (formerly JCPenney) has not been successful with its most recent rebranding (they've rebranded three times in the past few years, which is not good for customer loyalty either). In an effort to modernize, they got rid of something customers had grown to love about the brand: coupons. With its new "fair and square pricing," the company announced that sales and discounts were a thing of the past. As it turns out, that was simply too radical a change in JCP's branding foundation and customers revolted. As JCP came to discover, those very sales and coupons were what drove loyal customers into the stores, so now the sales are back.

A failed rebrand can be very damaging to a business, and it can take a long time to win back customers who've left. But at the same time, if you understand why the rebrand failed, it can help you define and hone your core values.

And sometimes rebranding works and gives a company an opportunity to grow its customer base and its long-term success. Few of you probably remember when Abercrombie & Fitch sold only fishing and hunting gear to sportsmen. That's right: it was the least cool store in the mall—in fact it wasn't even *in* the mall. Then the company rebranded not only their logo and marketing but their stores and products as well to appeal to a younger and hipper demographic. Suddenly, the hunting and fishing chain became competitive with the Gap and J. Crew. How did they pull it off? They tackled the entire business and changed it from the core values up.

Tabatha's Final Take: Own Your Brand

* Your brand is not about flashy logos or empty promises. It's about what you want people to think of when they hear your name. It represents the very best of who you are and what your business is about.

* Like everything else you have worked to create in your business, a brand takes time and effort. Make sure you don't just talk the talk—you need to walk the walk as well. You are the living embodiment of your brand (as are your employees). Everything you do and say should speak to what you are trying to convey in your brand messaging.

* Great brands resonate with us. They symbolize more than just a burger or a piece of clothing on a rack. They represent home, comfort, even the good life. Strive to create a brand that inspires fierce customer loyalty and commitment—something that the public wants/needs/ loves.

7

Clients

• •

"The truth is, we have relationships with our customers, each and every one of them. And like all relationships, we can have issues. Sometimes, I've had to 'fire' mine."

• •

I s the customer always right? That's a tricky question. It's become a standard service industry motto, but is it really true? A business only survives and thrives with happy, satisfied customers, and an owner should strive to make clients content. But what happens when a customer takes advantage? What do you do about the loudmouth who is rude or the chronic complainer who is never pleased? I'll tell you what I did . . .

I had a client at my salon who booked me every six weeks like clockwork. She would come in and tell me what she wanted, and I would give it to her. Before she left, she'd tell me how great her cut or style was and how much she loved it. But two days later, my phone would ring: "Tabatha," she'd say, "a piece fell out of place." Or, "Tabatha, the fringe is too long." I always invited her back and fixed her issue free of charge. But I had to break this pattern, so I asked her to bring in pictures so we would have a visual benchmark for her requested style. "Tear some out of magazines or print them off the Internet," I advised her. "Show me *exactly* how you want me to do it."

When we compared her final look to the photo she brought in, it was nearly identical. "It's perfect!" she announced. Then two days later, it wasn't perfect—and back she came for me to do yet another "fix."

Finally, after going through this cycle for several years, I decided enough was enough. It was time for a sit-down. It was time to fire my customer. I explained that it had become clear that I could not please her. "I think it's better if you find a hairdresser who can make you happy," I told her. I even offered to help her find one. She was stunned—as if this had come out of nowhere. "I'm always happy with your work!" she insisted.

After that, she continued to come back every six weeks and never complained again. She had an unrealistic expectation and she didn't realize it, so I had to let her know. It's a difficult situation; ultimately I want a customer to be happy. They deserve to be. But some people don't realize that they're habitual complainers.

There have been other times when I had to tell a customer to go elsewhere. I had to be okay with that loss and manage the process in a professional way. It's critical that you never get to a point where the parting of ways is unpleasant for either of you. This is what Owning Your Clients is about. If a client is chronically late, you need to let them know how that is affecting your schedule and give them the choice to remedy it. If a client is rude, you should explain the impact that it's having on your staff and let them change their behavior. The customer is always right to the extent that you should always try to preserve the owner/client relationship. But if that customer is hurting your business, it's not an acceptable situation for anyone.

Mind Your Own Business:
Coping with customers from hell

Let's do a little role-playing here. You're the boss . . . I'm the disgruntled client with a bone to pick. Every customer is valuable and needs to be valued. That said, some situations are more egregious than others, and they don't all warrant the same response. So I want you to practice how you would handle each situation. Let's take the example of a restaurant and look at these escalating customer service issues:

> *"Excuse me. I asked the waitress for my check fifteen minutes ago, and I haven't seen her since. And now I'm going to be late!"*

This is aggravating for the customer, but on a scale of issues, it is probably fixed with an apology and making sure it is corrected. "I'm so sorry, I will go get your check right now and make sure it is expedited."

> *"Your waitress totally screwed up my sandwich! I wanted rye bread, not white! And what the hell is this cheese? It's not Swiss! I said no mayo . . . I want mustard!"*

This is a bigger issue because not only has the customer not gotten the food he wanted but he is also now being left to wait for a new meal. This requires the customer to be compensated in some way so that he feels like he isn't paying for something he didn't get. "I apologize. Please, let me take that back to the kitchen and get you what you ordered. And, of course, this will be on us today."

"I told my waitress that she brought me the wrong sandwich and she insisted that this is what I ordered and walked away in a huff."

This is completely unacceptable. I would first deal with the customer, who needs to be compensated, so I would then correct the order and comp it. But additionally I would assure the customer that I will speak with the server. However, and this is very important, I would never reprimand staff in front of a customer. I see this a lot. A frustrated owner or manager tries to satisfy a disgruntled customer by yelling at the employee right there. It is unprofessional, sets a bad example, and embarrasses the other customers. Always take the employee to the back or outside, someplace private, and have a calm but firm conversation. This particular server's response probably warrants a sanction of some kind, given how unacceptable it is.

Norma's Notes: BE ON YOUR BEST BEHAVIOR

My mother ran a very different kind of business, one that needed the customers to be ruled with an iron fist. If one of the patrons at her clubs got drunk or unruly with one of the girls, my mother had zero tolerance. The customer was tossed out on his ear; it didn't matter how regular or important he was. This was appropriate and didn't negatively impact her business because the rules were clearly communicated. And the consequences if a patron broke a rule were also clearly communicated. If a customer got disorderly, it ruined everyone else's experience, which was unacceptable to . . . everyone else. And most important, bad behavior was a danger to the girls working in the bar, and that was completely unacceptable to my mother as their employer. She insisted on a safe working environment for them.

Tabatha's Ten Commandments of Customer Service

Although there are many customers who bitch, complain, and make unreasonable demands, you can't just say "Screw you!" and ignore them. Part of owning your customers is building a successful relationship with them. Loyalty has to be earned; it's work. Your clients will notice if you treat them with respect and courtesy. They will feel special and taken care of, and they will want to give you their business and hopefully spend more and more each time. If you invest in them, they will invest in you.

I suggest posting this list to remind you and your staff:

1. **Thou shalt be consistent.** You can't offer quality service just to woo in new customers then drop the ball. You have to keep the quality high and keep it up.

2. **Thou shalt provide value.** The customer should feel the experience has been worth the price and that they are totally satisfied with the product or service. In short: they got their money's worth.

3. **Thou shalt not employ someone who is clueless.** A customer wants someone who knows what they are talking about and can help them. I don't care what product or service you are offering, your staff should be on the ball and have the right information. More about this in the next chapter.

4. **Thou shalt be friendly.** Why would a customer keep coming back and spending money if your staff (and you) are rude and surly? You need to be genuine, polite, and respectful, and remember that customers can smell fake and disingenuous a mile away.

5. **Thou shalt not lie.** Customers want you to tell them the

truth. If you promise or claim something, you better deliver! If you don't, not only will they never return, but they'll tell all their friends to stay away, too. I always believe you are better to underpromise and overdeliver. Exceed a client's expectations and you'll make plenty of fans.

6. **Thou shalt not make excuses.** Customers don't care that your computer crashed, your shipment was late, or that your receptionist is sick. They want to know you will get the job done, handle the situation, and take care of them.

7. **Thou shalt care about your customer.** They need to feel like they are important and you care about their needs. If you prove that you are emotionally invested, then you will have a loyal customer for life.

8. **Thou shalt show your appreciation.** Customers want to know that you value their business and hard-earned money. Offer a rewards program, special discounts, priority booking, even a glass of champagne on the holidays. Everything will let them know they're loved.

9. **Thou shalt make it easy.** Convenience is key. Don't keep customers waiting, have well-organized displays, and have a Web site with current products/services and ways to book or order. Make absolutely certain that your location is convenient to your clientele. A high-traffic area may be more expensive, but it will pay off because it is easier for more people to patronize.

10. **Thou shalt clean up your act.** Customers want a clean, organized, fresh environment. No garbage lying around; no leftover lunches or personal crap littering the space. This is the first impression people get of your business, and if it's dirty, tired, or cluttered, it's a bad one that's difficult to erase.

CASE STUDY
The owner who ignored her guests

One way to test whether you have great customer service is to ask yourself, Is this how I would want to be treated? I have worked with many owners who completely neglect and alienate their clients. And when I ask them that question they give me a stunned no. So then why are they treating their customers—the people who are paying them so they can stay in business—that way?

It is all about hospitality. As a prime example, I worked with a bed-and-breakfast in Los Angeles where the customer service was atrocious. There were no basic gestures, big or small. In fact, they didn't even serve a breakfast (and isn't that the point of a bed-and-breakfast?). The owner didn't clean the guest's room unless they paid extra and didn't provide any amenities. She wasn't even there when the guest checked in—she just left a key under the mat, which was a major security problem.

"Why are you ignoring your customer service?" I asked her. She informed me that it was "enough" to open her home to strangers. Well, it wasn't enough. If I were a guest, I would have taken my bags and gotten the hell out of there! I didn't mince words. I told this owner she had to realize that her off-putting, snobbish personality was not "hospitable" and she needed to be more engaged and inviting. She was not putting any effort into her customer relations.

I had to teach her that her customers were literally her biggest assets. Their word of mouth could help bring in new customers more than any advertisement. In today's world, word of mouth isn't just telling a BFF or coworker where to go. It's posting positive or negative reviews on sites like Trip Advisor, Fodor's, or Hotels.com that are read by thousands. The owner seemed to finally see the light and realize that bringing a paying guest into her home was not unlike inviting a personal guest; all guests want to feel welcomed and comfortable. She even started serving breakfast!

Way too much information

Don't mistake my use of the word *relationship* as a signal that you should get all up in your customers' business. Crossing the line—such as sharing your personal information—is not acceptable. Neither is pumping your client for intimate info (as salacious as the details might be!) that they don't want to share. And you don't need to be offering free advice, either professional or personal. You are not their shrink. You are not their best friend. I don't care how many times a week you see them, keep your nose out of someone else's affairs.

That said, as a hairdresser and salon owner, my clients tend to share all kinds of personal moments and feelings with me. I simply say "How are you today?" and out it pours. I have been a sounding board for births, deaths, marriages, divorces, remarriages, and illnesses. Do I listen? Of course. It's polite and it shows I care, which I do. But I am always mindful that these are clients, not friends. I am there to provide a service, not offer my opinion. Do I think you should divorce your cheating husband? It doesn't matter. I am not the person you should be seeking counseling from. Obviously, if a client asks for recommendations for a good restaurant, clothing shop, or great mechanic, I share. But when someone wants to know how to handle a personal crisis, I refrain. I don't want to put my two cents' worth in and have it backfire. What happens if you tell a customer "Dump the cheating bum! He isn't good enough for you!" and she decides to give it another try? She may be too embarrassed (or pissed) to come in and face you ever again. I also find that most people don't really want you to tell them what to do even if they ask. They already know what the answer is, and they just want someone to bitch and vent to.

I always maintain a professional, not personal, relationship with my clients. I would never go out drinking with them, invite them into my house, or share details of my personal life with them. If you want to know about my life, read my books. It's not coming out of my mouth!

Extra, extra

After I bought my salon, my mother gave me a giant Costco bag of Starbursts. I put the candies into a jar by the front desk at my salon just to get rid of them. When the stash ran out, I removed the bowl. Sure enough, clients came in asking me where the Starbursts went. It was a minor extra that had enhanced their experience and they missed it. Who knew? From that moment on, there was always a bowl of Starbursts at my front desk. Owners need to find the gestures, big and small, that make their business unique to the customer and make him or her feel special. In my case, chewy rainbow candies did the trick.

But be careful how you go about these gestures because some of them can send the wrong message. Anyone who knows me knows I don't believe in coupons. Discounting your services or goods sends the wrong message; it cheapens what you do and sell. I would rather give away a service or product so that people have the opportunity to try it and then return to pay full price the next time. As far as rewarding loyal customers, I feel similarly. Loyalty shouldn't be rewarded with discounts, as that sends the message that your prices are too high in the first place. Loyalty should be rewarded over time with an extra service or free product. Build loyalty up over multiple visits or purchases and then reward it with something special, something the clients might not have bought for themselves.

There is a real science to this process. Owners need to track their clients' retention rates and spending habits. For top clients, make sure you reward them in other ways to foster loyalty. At my salon, I sent birthday cards and gave holiday gifts to top clients. I would also thank new clients with a card so that they felt that they were valued right out of the gate. Anything you can do to make a customer feel appreciated will foster that all-important relationship with them.

But once you start, don't get lazy. Slacking off on the perks is the worst thing you can do to your relationship with a client (remember how my customers freaked over the missing Starbursts!). Once you set expectations, you need to consistently meet them and even exceed them.

Tabatha's Final Take: Own Your Clients

✳ Treat your customer with respect and appreciation. The goal is to keep them coming back for more.

✳ That said, there will be some clients who abuse the relationship. Yes, you want to keep your client happy, but not at the expense of your business. If they are causing problems, sit down and politely and professionally let them know.

✳ Reward your customer with little extras: a bowl of candy at the front desk, a frequent-client program, a glass of bubbly to ring in the holidays.

✳ Never mistake a client for your BFF. Do not share details of your personal life, and refrain from giving them advice on personal matters.

8

Success

"I have never done something solely because I thought it would be financially successful. That can't be the only motive. I have always viewed success as accomplishing your greatest challenge. Set the bar at the highest point and know that when you meet that bar, you are successful."

There is no such thing as "How to Succeed in Business Without Really Trying." You have to work hard, all the time—and then some. And when you do and you see the respect you're gaining from your customers, employees, and fellow owners in your field, you'll know it's worth it. Anything worth having is worth busting your ass for.

That's why, when you finally earn success, you should Own It as much as you own everything else. I want you to learn how to embrace it, measure it, build on it, and reap the rewards. What does it mean to be successful? Some people measure success by the size of their bank account or by status symbols, the labels they wear or the cars they drive. Others measure success by their power and ability to control their circumstances. I define success by personal growth; if you don't continue to grow, you can't continue to succeed.

My definition of success is never standing still. Today's success doesn't guarantee tomorrow's results. I hate it when an owner simply sits back and rests on his or her laurels. Emerson had it wrong: a foolish complacency, not consistency, is the hobgoblin of little minds. Owning Your Success is always thinking about what to do next. Is it time to raise the bar higher? Branch out? I'll tell you what it's *not* time to do: sit around counting your money. Because what you *can* count on is that things won't stay this way forever.

CASE STUDY
The bar that believed it was the best

I worked with a bar in Long Beach, California. It had been *the* gay bar to visit for years, but by the time I got there, that reputation was long gone. The owners were stuck in a time warp! They dwelled on the success they once had and blamed everyone else for their failures—it was their staff's fault for not following their rules; it was their customers' fault for not liking how they ran things; it was their competitions' fault for being competitive. They refused to own up to the fact that everything had changed except them. And when I asked what was going on, I got a lot of bragging and boasting based on how things used to be: "We're so good! We're the best in the area. Nobody can do it like us!"

I quickly realized that this wasn't denial about how bad their situation was, but actually arrogance based on how successful they *used* to be. They couldn't understand why what made them successful in 1979 or 1985 wasn't working today. But the truth is, they hadn't seen a good week in a long, long time. It took a lot of work to get them to see that their old ideas no longer worked and that they needed to try new ideas. I took the owners and staff to one of the top gay bars in L.A. so they could see how a new generation built success. Thankfully, the light-bulb finally went off. They let go of the glory days from the past and did what needed to be done. They agreed to change their rules, their drinks, and their attitude, and now the bar is back on top. Today they aren't just reveling in glory days that have past but are also building success that can live on.

Look to the future

Owning Your Success goes hand in hand with Owning Your Future. I believe you should always be thinking big picture and looking down the road. Even if things are beyond fabulous at this moment in time, don't assume they will be next month, five years from now, or even ten years from now. I am constantly setting new goals of what I would like to accomplish. But let's be real here: no one has a crystal ball. While you can try to stay ahead of trends, innovations, and even personal changes, you will still need one key quality to truly be successful: you need to be able to adapt. The most successful people I know are also the most flexible.

I would be lying if I told you I have never deviated from my best-laid plans. I believe you jump on an opportunity when it presents itself—and you adapt your plan accordingly. I did not plan to do a television show, but when the opportunity arose, I took advantage of it. In retrospect, I'm glad I did, because it helped grow my career in a new direction I hadn't planned for. In fact, I ended up selling my salon and focusing on building new success around my new career choice to build a brand through television and media. That would not have happened if I hadn't been open to responding to a casting notice calling hairdressers to apply for a TV show called *Shear Genius.*

When I go into troubled businesses, many owners will torture me by insisting their plan was working. Maybe it was, but now it isn't, or I wouldn't be there. If it were still working, I wouldn't have taken your keys and read you the riot act. There comes a time when you have to switch gears and change. It's called adapting. It doesn't mean you're a failure—quite the opposite. It means you're flexible and capable of readjusting your plan because it needs it. You are open to change and you understand that it brings new opportunity. Successful people don't resist change; they embrace it head-on. Every loss is a chance to win. Every mistake is a chance to grow. Unless, of course, you prefer to be a stubborn mule—in which case, I will probably be paying you a visit very soon and taking your keys.

Believe me: I get it. I am a person who loves control, and sudden change can feel like a total loss of control. No one likes to feel the ground shaking beneath them. But here's my advice: roll with it. Change can bring your greatest success if you're open to it.

Mind Your Own Business: How do I define success?

This is an exercise that will help you set the bar for what success means to you. I want you to make a list of all the things you want to accomplish—professionally as well as personally. You can list your goals for the rest of your lifetime or just for over the next few years. I find that putting goals down on paper really makes them stick. Remember that success isn't always about achievement. Sometimes it's simply getting through the day, executing your vision, or staying calm in a storm. Often it's not about money, fame, or power but instead about feeling safe, secure, and sane. There's no right or wrong here—this is your list. Maybe it includes . . .

* Love what I do and do what I love.
* Grow my business to include a second/third/fourth store.
* Build a name for myself and a solid reputation in my field.
* Learn to balance my checkbook and understand finances.
* Be able to afford a nanny so I have more time for me.
* Buy a new car so I have reliable transportation.
* Put away enough money to send my kids to college.
* Be able to retire when I'm fifty-five—and live comfortably in my golden years.

Don't be scared of success

Some people are actually afraid of their own success and will, whether consciously or unconsciously, try to sabotage themselves. Don't stand in your own way. I have a friend who can't keep a job for more than a year. There is always something wrong with her boss, her clients, the location, etc. She finds a reason to leave the salon and move on. And as a result she always has to start over, in the worst chair, recruiting new clients, building new relationships with her boss and coworkers. She can't get ahead because she blocks herself at every turn. You might wonder why anyone would do this when it is so clearly counterproductive. I have one word for you: *fear*. These people live in terror of the prospect of failing. So to prevent that from happening, they shoot themselves down before they even get close to succeeding. It's a control thing.

So here is the advice I gave to this friend: your biggest failure is not caused by your work situation. It's caused by your own hesitation to stay somewhere and build your success one step at a time. Part of what I mean when I say Own Your Success is: make a commitment. You have to be committed to your career and your business to make it successful. You can't run away when things get tough. That's when you should get tough as well.

I've also met my share of pessimists who simply declare, "I can't be successful." That negative attitude may just prove them right! Anyone—I repeat—anyone can be successful if they are pragmatic, proactive, and determined. I've seen people grow billion-dollar empires out of nothing. Owning Your Success is allowing yourself to be successful, which requires some optimism about what is possible in the future. Every time your inner critic says "I can't" or "I won't," you are not owning success.

People will tell me they don't "deserve" success. To that I say, get over it. Stop feeling guilty and insecure. If you've worked your tail off to get where you are, then don't apologize. Other people worry that success will "change them." They'll lose friends or they won't have the same life they're used to living. They're comfortable hanging out at the bar with their unemployed friends bitching about the world. Yes, if you're successful, it's possible that your life may change. Friends are friends, no matter what phase you are going through. If they dump you over a job (or you have to dump them), then they weren't worth your time in the first place.

Don't let it go to your head

I can't stand people who are successful and feel the need to rub everyone's nose in it. Whatever happened to humility? In my humble opinion (and I do believe I am fairly humble), part of Owning Your Success is learning how to handle it. Success can blind you. When all you can see is how far you've come, you lose perspective on what it takes to stay there. As hard as it was to get on top, it's even harder to stay there. And I promise you, if you buy into your own press and lose your work ethic, you'll come crashing down. Even worse, thanks to your big mouth, no one will be there to catch you.

The owner of the first salon where I worked, in New Jersey, had started, built, and expanded a very successful business. He understood how to be personable with the clients and professional but fair with his staff. He cared about his business, and that came across to the clients and employees. Then he retired and his son took over. The son was a hairdresser, but he didn't have to work hard to build the business; he inherited it. And he took it all for granted and cared only about himself. He was aloof with the clients and egotistical with the staff, and it showed. And it didn't take long for the customers to start to go elsewhere and for the staff to find new jobs. While the salon is still open, it is a completely different place and doesn't have the loyalty that his father had built. Part of Owning Your Success is being humble and remembering what is important to a successful business, which is focusing on clients and staff and not on yourself. I want you to look at how you address success even on a daily basis. When your sales go up slightly, do you share the credit with your hardworking staff or partners? When you turn a profit for the first time, do you thank your family and friends for all their love and support (and perhaps repay their loans)? Or do you simply say "I'm hot shit!" and let it go to your head, where it's bound to take up too much room? Make sure you are Owning It—not *abusing it*. Because eventually you will come crashing down, and all those friends and employees will be too fed up with your arrogant attitude to help you again.

It's fine to take pride in what you've achieved. I take pride in what I do. But you need to share credit where credit is due, and you should talk honestly—not arrogantly—about your accomplishments. It's great to be optimistic about your future, and there is nothing wrong with a little self-promotion—as long as it is honest and accurate. I don't believe in "fake it until you make it," a phrase I hear all the time and have come to loathe. Never lie, and don't build a plan on faking anything. Do the hard work to deserve the accolades, whether they are from yourself or others. A fraud is always found out. Remember, the proof is in the pudding. Clients may try out your business based on your promotion, but you always need to deliver and even overdeliver to keep them coming back. All the self-promotion in the world doesn't matter if you don't do the work to retain those new customers.

Another major mistake people make is defining their success

by putting down the competition and pointing out their failures. Trashing someone's reputation is both bad form and bad karma. If you can't talk about the positive attributes that your business has without going negative on the marketplace, you will not be so successful after all. The biggest turnoff for any potential or new customer is hearing you bad-mouth a competitor. It only shows how insecure (and probably inferior) you are.

Norma's Notes:

MOM WOULD HAVE BEEN PROUD

Another part of Owning Your Success is identifying your champions and keeping them close when you are nervous or scared. They will help you rally and remember that you can accomplish the task no matter how intimidating.

The year after my mother passed away, I did my first red carpet event for the Oscars. It was bittersweet because I was excited to do it but disappointed my mother was not around to see me. I knew she would have been so proud of me. She was a fan of movies and movie stars, but she also thought I was a star. Even when I was that chubby little kid with no friends, my mother told me that someday I would be a star.

As I prepared to stand on the carpet that day, I was a bundle of nerves. So I thought about what Norma would have said to calm me down. She would have told me that I would be brilliant. To my mother, being on the red carpet at the Oscars, especially as a critic talking about the stars, would have been the ultimate symbol of success, and I let that notion encourage me to go out and do my best.

Tabatha's Final Take: Own Your Success

✳ Success can do funny things to people. It can make you fearful and derail your own efforts. It can make you turn into a pompous ass. Owning it means learning how to handle it in a way that will continue to grow your business and keep you succeeding over the long term.

✳ There is nothing worse than someone who rests on his/her laurels. So you've accomplished something . . . so what? What will you do next? Time to set the bar even higher!

✳ Define what success means to you—not what it means to everyone else. It will help you stay on track with your plans if you know what the ultimate goal is. It may be money, fame, or power, or it may be something different that is just as important to you.

PART III

Own Your Network

9

Personal Relationships

. . . .

"I have always believed that you teach people how to treat you. If you act like a victim, people will treat you like one. If you act like a winner, people will treat you like one. We all need to put out the energy that we want to get back."

. . . .

I have a single friend who had been desperately looking for love. She had gone to every singles event, signed up for every dating service, all to no avail. Just when she decided to stop the search and focus on her career, Mr. Right showed up. Why? Because she stopped putting out that desperate "I need a man" energy and replaced it with "I like myself" energy. And suddenly, he appeared. The fact is, he was there the whole time, but the shift in her energy *attracted* him to her.

Another woman I know had a knack for attracting losers: men who used her, abused her, then cheated on her or robbed her blind. Time and time again, she replayed these same patterns. No one could convince her of this; she had to learn it for herself. Everyone does, and that's part of Owning It. There has to be a point where you say, "Enough is enough. I'm tired of being around people who don't treat me the way I want to be treated." If you have had your share of lousy relationships, it's time to examine why and what it says about you. If you're stuck in a pattern of alliances (both personal and professional) that drain your energy and make you feel unhappy and unappreciated, you need to stop it here and now. No more whining or crying—by now you know I have no patience for that. The key to owning your personal relationships is action rather than reaction.

Mind Your Own Business: Finding positivity

When I go into a business that is broken, I am always searching for something positive in the situation—and I teach owners and staff members to do the same. For this exercise, I want you to look for positivity outside of yourself: people, places, things, and situations. Try for at least three a day. It can be good news: a friend who's gotten engaged; a nephew who got into the college of his choice; a new restaurant opening in your neighborhood. It can be something that inspires you: a great quote; a random act of kindness; even a rainbow, if it puts a smile on your face. The point of this exercise is to train yourself to recognize and focus on the positive. At first, finding three might be tough. But the more you do it every day, the easier it gets. I recommend you keep a running list in a journal or in your phone's notepad. Refer to it whenever you feel yourself sliding back down a dark hole.

Next, I want you to try to look for the positive in a difficult or stressful situation. When you encounter an issue that might take you to a place of anger, frustration, or defeat, force yourself to face it with a different approach. Try to be optimistic, solution oriented, and collaborative. If you can focus on positivity inside and out, you will improve your relationship with yourself and inevitably with others.

Fool me twice, shame on me

Even if you don't believe in the law of attraction, you can understand that people often get trapped in a vicious cycle. Once you've established bad patterns in your relationships, it can be very tough to break them. But that's exactly what you must do. It's a waste of time, energy, and brain cells to repeat the same mistake twice.

The problem is, we will just keep repeating our bad patterns in relationships if we don't change ourselves first. The vicious cycle of picking one wrong person after another can only be broken if you step away and focus on the part of yourself that is driving you to make bad choices. First of all, if you want to avoid repeating your mistakes, you need to learn from them. This requires you to look at your relationships objectively and critically. What are you doing wrong that you could be doing right? Why are you attracted to particular types of people? Are you articulating what you want and need? Are you open to different kinds of people who will bring new and potentially positive elements into your life? The good news is, once you identify and own your patterns, you are that much closer to changing them for the better.

Everyone has baggage. You need to figure out how it affects you and if it's keeping you locked into repeating a bad pattern. My dad abandoned me and my mother, and that clearly affected how I trust (or distrust) people. I'm usually not easily drawn into a friendship. I tend to be hypervigilant of people's underlying intentions and more than a little suspicious. But I am aware of these tendencies and have tried to turn them into positive attributes. People tell me I am an astute judge of character, and I am sure my difficult childhood is one reason why.

This is why I get mad at myself when I have poor or clouded judgment. My mother saw this one coming from a mile away: she warned me that a very close work friend wasn't genuine and was jealous of my success. I didn't listen because I thought this person was a true friend. Of course, as she predicted, he eventually turned on me and abandoned the friendship. If I had listened to her, I probably would have saved myself not only the pain of his betrayal but also the aggravation I felt for not seeing it.

CASE STUDY
Mr. Wrong showed me what was right for me

Bad relationships aren't always bad—not if they teach us something and help us grow up and move on. One of my past romantic relationships was with an American pro-ball player. We dated for almost two years, and when it ended (with the hood of his Porsche wrecked), I realized I had repeated my mother's pattern. I had let a man treat me badly, cheat on me, and not make a real commitment to me. From that point on, I have never dated someone like this again. I broke the pattern; I learned what it was that I wanted and needed. Since then, the people I have chosen have been more giving and caring, and I have had more equal romantic relationships. The break-up may be messy and painful, but if it spares you some future hurt and gives you a much-needed wake-up call, I'd say it wasn't all bad.

Set your boundaries

No relationship can exist without boundaries. Even the people you love the most need to have some ground rules. Probably the hardest boundaries and expectations to set are in your relationships with family members. I have three half brothers who are all older than me, and therefore, I haven't always had the closest relationships with them. But over the years, I wanted to improve our connection, especially a strained relationship with one of them. We hadn't seen each other in twelve years when I took a trip home to Australia. I decided to go to his house to see him and his children, and he proceeded to tell me that he was "okay with me being around the kids" but he would not let them watch my TV show because I am "a nasty bitch on it." In the meantime, they were sitting there watching an episode of *Toddlers & Tiaras,* which (no disrespect to Honey Boo Boo) isn't exactly a bastion of educational programming.

My brother's attitude was annoying, but I let it pass. Then, when my mother got sick, I called everyone in the family so they could say their final good-byes. My brother kept telling me he didn't know what to say to her. When they finally did speak, all he could muster was "travel safe."

After she died, he didn't contact me for a long time. He never checked in to see how I was doing. Two years later, out of the blue, he messaged me and explained that someone he worked with loved my show. He wanted me to Facebook this person to confirm that I was in fact his sister. I assume so he could look like a big shot and use me to impress people.

I was floored. Wasn't I the sister he preferred to distance himself and his family from? As you can imagine, that was the final straw in a relationship that has never been positive or functional, no matter how hard I tried. I finally understood that I had allowed him to behave this way and that I needed to draw the line in the sand. No more! I finally set a firm boundary, and unfortunately, my brother and I will not speak again unless he changes dramatically.

I don't recommend that anyone let a relationship get to such a bad place. In my case, what was sadly missing in our sibling relationship was communication (and not for any lack of effort on my part). Having a sit-down isn't as tough as you think if both parties are ready and willing. You want to try to talk with that person from a positive place, about how the relationship can improve, as opposed to from a place of anger or exasperation. In other words, don't have this conversation in a moment of frustration and don't let the relationship get to such a bad place that you can't be positive.

When you are ready to talk, express yourself clearly, concisely, and honestly. Sometimes the truth hurts, but silence is the real relationship killer. If you've decided to open up the floodgates in order to get a relationship back on track, then here's how:

• Avoid name-calling. I'm going to have a very difficult time hearing what you're saying if you precede it with "You're a major fuckup." How would you like to be spoken to? Then that is how you should address anyone you are in a relationship with. You can think it; just don't say it.

- See his/her perspective. There are two sides to every argument. Consider the other person's point of view. Where is the problem stemming from? What feelings are behind it?

- Find the right time to talk. Timing is everything. If you want to have it out with your spouse, over dinner with his parents is probably not ideal. Find a time when you are both relaxed, not distracted, and not exhausted. Privacy is also a plus. It's not the best idea to air your grievances at the grocery store checkout or in front of the kids.

- Keep your cool. I am not the best at this; I do tend to blow my top when pushed to my limits. My advice is to keep your voice down if and when you can. Shouting instantly ups the aggression and puts the other person on the defensive. Instead, take a deep breath. Think about what you want to say and how you want to say it. If you're so angry you can't see straight, then take a walk around the block and come back to the conversation later. It's hard to take back things we say in anger—sometimes, impossible.

- Don't play the blame game. It's not one person's fault if the relationship is troubled. I promise you that somewhere, somehow, both of you have managed to screw this up. Phrases like "This is all your fault!" will get you nowhere. Instead, make this about how *you* feel, such as, "When you ignored my calls yesterday, it made me feel sad and worried." Slight change of wording, big difference in communicating.

- Apologize. We're going to discuss owning your mistakes in chapter 14. But for now, let me leave you with this advice. If you fucked things up, then say you're sorry. We all make mistakes in relationships, and you need to acknowledge this. Suck it up. Ditch the ego and admit you're wrong if indeed you were. If you weren't, I don't advise just tossing out apologies left and right to smooth things over. That's just a Band-Aid, not a long-term solution.

And once you have gotten everything off your chest, talked it through, and hopefully set some new boundaries and expectations, let it go! I can't stress this strongly enough. Rehashing the past in new arguments is a sure relationship killer. No one wants to feel like their spouse, friend, or business partner is keeping some kind of lifetime list of their transgressions. If you are prepared to continue the relationship, then you need to be prepared to put the issues that are resolved to bed.

Norma's Notes:
THE MOTHER/DAUGHTER RELATIONSHIP

My mother and I were very close. We lived together most of my life, we traveled together, and we talked about everything. But I never forgot that she was my mother because she never let me. She would call me out, tell me off, but also give me advice and comfort me like no one else. I was very respectful of her, and at times, I feared her. We had boundaries and we knew what they were. She was the mother and I was her daughter.

I often hear women say that they are "friends" with their daughters, and I think that is problematic. Friends do not have the same boundaries or rules as do mothers and daughters. A mother knows best. A friend does not. Children need to know who is the boss and have someone to look up to and keep them in line. Friends do not serve that same purpose. Telling your child that you are their friend and then trying to exercise authority is very challenging. God knows what my mother would have had to say about it!

Tabatha's Final Take:
Own Your Personal Relationships

❅ You get back what you put out there. If you want to attract positive people into your life, then project that energy. If you advertise desperation and depression, you're going to lure in every loser on the block, like flies to garbage!

❅ To own your personal relationships you must first know yourself better than anyone else does. No one can make you happy or treat you how you want/need to be treated unless you understand what makes you tick.

❅ Even lousy relationships can have a good outcome. See your mistakes for what they truly are: life lessons.

❅ Set your boundaries, even with those closest to you. No one gets free rein or carte blanche in your life.

❅ People treat you how you allow them to.

❅ Communication, honesty, and respect are the keys to both personal and professional relationships. No exceptions.

Work Relationships

10

*"I have worked for some great bosses and some not-so-great ones.
But they have all helped to shape me into the boss and leader
I am today. Everyone can benefit from working their way up to
being the boss. There is a lot to be learned from working for someone else and learning the ropes."*

Just because you own a business that has a bunch of employees doesn't mean you actually have a team. Building a team takes work, and a lot of owners and managers have no idea how to do this. When I first came to the United States from London my boss was a man who was very involved in his salon business. He worked hard to grow it, triple its size, and increase its staff. He was a charismatic guy and appreciated both his clients and the people who worked for him. He knew all his staff by name and would walk around the salon saying hello to everyone and checking in. He knew many of the regular clients' names also, and he would make a point of welcoming them and complimenting their hair. I worked for him for about five years when he decided it was time to pass the torch on to his son, who was a hairdresser but the total opposite of his dad. He wasn't invested in the business because it was already successful.

It was difficult for me to go from a boss who cared so greatly about his staff to one who didn't even take the time to get to know us. And when he did get to know us, he played favorites—typically the "good" employees were his friends and the rest of us were the castoffs. If that wasn't enough to divide the team, he was also cheap in the way he ran the salon, which made the staff feel even more disregarded and poorly treated. In the end, it was an important lesson: this was not how I would treat my employees when I became a boss. I understood why we had been a team under his dad and why we came apart at the seams under him. And I knew I wanted to make sure my employees were a team.

I would own my staff. Just cutting them a paycheck and giving them a place to work is not enough. You have to care. You have to give them structure and set expectations. You have to be a leader in every sense of the word. Yes, this chapter is about the people who work for you. But it's really about you—how you treat them, and how you keep them in line but also happy and helping you achieve the goals of your business.

It all begins with the boss

Average employees only become great employees one way: leadership. A group of disparate individuals needs a leader to make them a team. This raises the question: what is good leadership? It starts with leading by example. Don't expect your staff to do something if you're not doing it yourself. I met a boss who was chronically late, and guess what happened? Her staff became chronically late. And what was the first thing she told me irritated her about her staff? "They were chronically late." And what was the first thing her employees told me irritated them? That their boss criticized them for being late when she was always late herself. This ridiculous viscous circle could only be broken one way. Docking their pay? No. Firing them? No. The boss needed to change her behavior. Only then would her staff respect her rules and feel compelled to follow them.

Absolutely every single thing you ask or require of your staff you must also be willing to do yourself. This doesn't mean you need to do their jobs, but it does mean you should know how to and you should be willing to pitch in when necessary. It also means you need to abide by all of the same rules, and you must be consistent. Many owners try to justify their bad behavior by telling me, "Yeah, but I am the boss." But all that their employees see is a boss who is lazy and two-faced. You can't exempt yourself just because you're in charge. A great boss . . .

- Follows the rules, all of the rules, all of the time.

- Says what she means and means what she says. Empty threats and empty promises to staff never work.

- Would never demand anything of his staff that he would not demand of himself.

- Rewards hard work and exemplary behavior as often as she penalizes or docks bad behavior.

- Connects with employees: asks them what they need, how he can help them, and reminds them that they are a valuable asset to this business.

- Doesn't burden employees with personal problems. They don't need to know that your car won't start or that you couldn't pay the rent this month. When you're having a bad day or your business is having issues, you need to do everything you can to *not* bring that to the workplace.

• Is a leader . . . not a buddy. I have seen many owners divest their authority and become "one of the gang" or friends with their employees. Danger, danger! This will erode all boundaries, and your staff will never listen to you or respect you. Even worse, you will wind up incredibly hurt every time they disappoint you, because you will take it personally instead of keeping it professional.

• Is present and accountable. You can't be a good boss if you're never there. I have no patience for the absentee boss. Managing your staff must be a hands-on process. If you don't have the time/energy to dedicate to your business's day-to-day running, you shouldn't be in business in the first place.

CASE STUDY
The partners who played good cop/bad cop

In order for your staff to feel like a team, they need to have clear expectations that they believe they are being set up to achieve. When a business has more than one boss, it can be more challenging to stay consistent in the messaging. Early in my career, I worked for a couple who owned a salon in Australia. Their dynamic was problematic: he was the good cop to whom all the employees went if they wanted something, while his wife was the boss who would reverse her husband's decision with great ire. If that wasn't enough to undermine a team, when the husband got wind of his wife's reversal, he would make fun of her in front of the employees, and she would then do the same to him. Ultimately the employees didn't respect either one of them and were more concerned about not getting caught in their dysfunction and/or gaming the system than doing a great job. Just like parents, owners need to always be on the same page, speak with a unified voice, and check in with each other before they make decisions about the team.

Hiring your dream team

The people you employ can make or break your business, so you want to hire smart. I don't have a perfect record of hiring the former. But I do think that I have honed my employee "radar" over the years. And I've devised a way for weeding them out in an interview. Never, I repeat, never hire anyone (not even your best friend's sister's neighbor who comes highly recommended) without interviewing them first. It's the only way to assess if they are the right fit, and it will spare you and them the aggravation of having to let them go later.

When someone walks in for an interview there are several key criteria, from small to large, for deciding if they are the right fit for your business:

- **How do they introduce themselves?** Do they have a firm handshake? Do they exude confidence? Are they personable, especially if they will be working in customer service?

- **Did they bring their résumé?** Are there typos? Are they prepared to discuss their work history in detail? Have they changed jobs too frequently? Have they been promoted consistently? Do they have the right skill set and knowledge for the position?

• Are they giving stock answers to interview questions? I like to throw in a couple of curveballs to loosen up a candidate and get them speaking freely and honestly.

• Do they ask appropriate questions about your business and you? They should be as invested in finding the right fit as you are. You need to be clear about the job description and your expectations. Don't sugarcoat it. The candidate should feel like they are getting what they bargained for if they are hired.

• How do they present themselves? Appearance matters, and if someone wants to make a good impression they should be mindful of their personal grooming. It is an extension of how professional they will be in your business.

• It is important to follow up an interview by checking on references. I can't tell you how many owners I meet who admit they never bothered to check references, and it often leads to a whole world of regret.

But in the end, the best advice I can give is the most subjective: trust your gut. Sometimes you get a feeling about someone that you can't put your finger on. Maybe they have all the wrong work experience on paper, but you pick up on their energy and enthusiasm and hire them anyway. And they become your star employee. Conversely, maybe someone has all the right answers, and that makes you feel uneasy, like the other shoe is about to drop. You may decide to hold out for someone who gives you a sense of ease and security instead.

Just asking

The interview is a great way to assess if a person will fit with your business before you actually hire them. The trick is to pose the right questions that coax out honest and revealing answers. I like to organize the interview into six parts. It's a pretty tough interrogation, but by the end, I'm confident if the person is a "go" or a "no."

Part 1: The intro

The answers to these questions will help you see what makes this person tick and whether you two will click.

- What are your hobbies/passions?
- What makes you stand out from others?
- What do you love about your job?
- What was the most challenging part of your last job?
- Why do you want to work here?

Part 2: Group dynamics

These questions will help you learn if he/she is a loner or a team player.

- Have you ever had to work with others to resolve a situation or get a task completed?
- What is the hardest thing about working with other people or being part of a team?
- What is the best thing about being part of a team?
- Do you prefer teamwork or working individually to complete a task?

• Have you had issues with management in previous jobs?

• Has there been a team member you haven't gotten along with? Why, and how did you handle it?

Part 3: Under fire
These questions will show you how a candidate copes with conflict.

• What would you do if you saw an employee doing something against company policy?

• Have you had to deal with an upset customer? What happened, and how did you handle it?

• What were some problems/complications in your last job? How did you handle them?

Part 4: The future
These responses reveal how motivated the candidate is.

• Tell me about your biggest accomplishments.

• What has been the best feedback you have ever received, and what did you learn from it?

• Where do you see your career going?

• What goals do you have for the future?

Part 5: Industry insider
The answers to these questions should tell you if the candidate has the skill and knowledge needed.

• What skills are your strongest?

• What skills are your weakest?

- How long have you been working in this industry?

- Where did you study/apprentice/work?

- Have you had additional training? Where and when?

- Do you consider yourself an expert in anything?

Part 6: The wrap-up

This is a great way to gauge if they've done their homework and how "into" this job they are.

- Does this position sound like something you'd be interested in? Why?

- What is it about my business that appeals to you?

- Do you have any questions for me?

CASE STUDY
The owner who hired her bestie

I have seen way too many owners make their staffing decisions based on emotional relationships instead of skill and job experience. I worked with a salon where the owner wasn't a stylist and, frankly, didn't have a clue about what to do. Instead of taking the time to hire a manager who knew the industry and could help her, she asked her best friend and her friend's twenty-one-year-old daughter to run her business. Beyond the personal relationship, this "manager" duo had no idea about the industry or the skills needed. You can imagine the resentment among the staff. The situation was killing the staff's morale, and even worse, it was costing the owner money because of their bad decisions. Her BFF was spending money on all the wrong things, which was killing her business. After I insisted that she spend more time understanding her business and getting to know her staff, she finally saw the main issue. Ultimately she decided she needed to fire her bestie and her daughter, which wasn't an easy thing for her to do, but in the end, it was the right choice. You always need to put the well-being of your business first.

Now that you understand how to hire the right employees, let's discuss how to turn them into a great team. A lot of businesses have high staff turnover, and high turnover has a negative impact on a business because customers like to see familiar faces and build a rapport with their service people. Staff usually leave because they don't feel like they are part of a team and/or they don't feel any loyalty. Owners need to make employees feel appreciated and satisfied and build loyalty to keep them around. To retain staff, you need to focus on the following:

Great expectations

You tell your employee you are unhappy, and she stares at you, dumbfounded. "I didn't know you wanted me to do that!" Who's right and who's wrong here? Is she an idiot—or did you not make your expectations clear?

Don't expect your staff to be mind readers. The most important thing you can do is set clear expectations. Everyone needs to know what is expected of them, as well as receive regular updates on whether they are meeting, exceeding, or failing those expectations. The expectations you set should be high but not impossible to achieve. I can't tell you how often I have had an employee claim a boss is never satisfied. They clean the stockroom and the boss wants it to be cleaned twice. Make sure you are realistic in your expectations, as well as in your assessments. And berating your team is not the answer; clarifying and demonstrating is. Show them how you like things done and allow for a learning curve. I always tell bosses to encourage rather than discourage.

Training

Contrary to what many owners think, good staff want to be well trained. They crave learning how to do their jobs better and being stimulated by exciting new ideas. If you don't train your staff properly then you are setting them up for failure, and no one likes to fail. One of my biggest pet peeves is walking into a store and asking a question only to be told, "I don't know." If you have staff working in your business, you need to make sure that they know everything about that business, and you need to make sure that if they don't have an answer they know exactly where to find it quickly. Customers want a sense of security, which results when staff have expertise; they assume it is part of what they are paying for. If they don't get it, that reflects poorly on the employee and on you.

Training is a business expense that truly pays off, and it is an ongoing commitment. You can't simply offer one training session and never do it again. I have worked with countless businesses that either put untrained employees in positions they shouldn't be in or have employees who haven't worked on their skills or taken a class in years. In both cases, it means the same: their work is subpar. Both of these situations are bad and can ruin your business.

CASE STUDY
The nail salon that knew nothing

Training doesn't consist of just handing employees a manual. Show as well as tell, and ideally, allow for hands-on participation. I worked with a nail salon where the owner wasn't a nail technician. She had no idea what it took to be one, which is why her business was failing. Few clients ever came back, and there were constant complaints about the poor quality of the manicures. She told me she had no idea why. Well, I knew why: the technicians' work was beyond bad. When I asked what training and experience the girls had, they told me they barely knew the basics. They were practicing their skills on paying clients! The owner believed that telling her staff to look at nail magazines or go online in their spare time was enough to teach them what they needed to know. Not so. They needed education and hands-on practice. Her lack of investing in training was the demise of her business. And I have to say . . . I saw it coming.

Depending on your profession, I recommend that bosses offer training weekly to every few months. The world is always changing, and your business needs to change along with it to stay current. That means learning the latest info and putting it to good use. Make sure your employees understand how this training can be used in their day-to-day work. This isn't just an FYI program; it's FYU: for your use. This is also an opportunity for job growth; the better they are, the farther they will go. There are several ways to implement training for your staff.

- Train on-site. You can have a manager or more experienced employee run a miniclass. I've known businesses that set up after-work, early-morning, or lunchtime training programs. An expert (for example, an experienced hairstylist) comes in to demonstrate and teach the latest techniques.

- Train off-site. Are local professional organizations or colleges offering a class? Is there a yearly conference in your field? Pay for it and send them. It's not an expense; it's an investment.

- Train online. In this high-tech world, there are also many online courses and "webinars" you can offer your employees. But don't expect them to simply hone their skills watching YouTube! Organize formal courses.

- Create a "partner"/"mentor" program. Pair a more experienced employee with a less experienced one so he/she can learn.

Compensation

A majority of Americans have to work very hard just to be able to make ends meet to support themselves. Remember this. And pay attention to the likely disparity between what you take home as an owner and what you pay your staff. I am not saying you don't deserve a great living, but I am saying that one of the ways an employee feels valued is through compensation. Your base wage must be competitive or even better than the market rate if you want to get the best people. It really is true that you get what you pay for when it comes to the people you employ. Strive to pay for the best. And incentivize them with bonuses or raises whenever you can afford to. Employee compensation is most often the highest percentage of a business's costs, but it is worth it if you get the right people.

Appreciation

Compensation isn't the only way to make an employee feel valued. And it isn't always the most effective way. A pat on the back goes a long way, and these compliments can actually be institutionalized through simple programs like "employee of the month." I worked with one salon owner who never appreciated his staff and was always disappointed in his product sales. I suggested that whenever a stylist sold a certain dollar amount of product in a month, he put their name on a board in the staff area so that they could be recognized and give them a gift certificate to someplace they enjoyed. His sales went through the roof, and his staff became more loyal than ever before.

Also, never underestimate the words *thank you*. When an employee does something that pleases you, acknowledge it. I don't hand out praise easily—it has to be well deserved. But when I do, I am sincere. And make sure you dole out your appreciation evenly and equally to all of your team. You never want to play favorites with a thank-you.

Mind Your Own Business: My rulebook

I want you to sit down and pen at least ten hard-and-fast rules you expect everyone in your business (including you) to follow. Consider the entire day from start to finish, and be as specific as possible. Is there a place you want the staff to hang up their coats and bags? Is there a time when they can take a lunch break? Should cell phones be silenced during the work period? Here are the top ten things that I expect from my employees.

1. Be punctual. If you're late, don't bother turning up. Unless there is a major transportation breakdown (such as all buses, trains, and cabs are unavailable), do not give me excuses. Lateness = laziness in my book.

2. Be polite. Treat your coworkers and clients with respect. Save the rude comments or frustrated exclamations for home.

3. Be honest. If you screwed up, own it. I am more understanding of someone who tells the truth than of someone who tries to cover it up with lies.

4. Be motivated. Take the initiative. Show me you are thinking on your feet and that you and I are working together to make this business successful.

5. Have a positive attitude. If you bring your problems or negative attitude to work every morning, you are not winning any points with me. Be bright and eager to work, learn, and help.

6. Look your best. By this I mean dress properly, neatly, and exhibit good hygiene. You are representing my business, so you better look the part.

7. Be a problem solver. I have the utmost respect for someone who doesn't just bitch and moan about problems but actually comes to me with ideas on how to fix them.

8. Be a team player. I am working hard to cultivate a team culture, so I don't tolerate shit stirrers. Throwing your coworkers under the bus? Refusing to shoulder your part of the load? Not cool. Be a team player . . . or play elsewhere.

9. Exhibit self-discipline. Despite temptation and impulse, I expect you to act like a mature and responsible individual at all times. No shopping on eBay or checking Facebook while waiting for your clients to arrive. There is surely a better use of your time and skill.

10. Show loyalty. I expect my employees to do right by the team and the business. We are in this together, and that means you don't bail on me the minute things go wrong—or a competitor offers you one dollar more an hour.

Norma's Notes: LOYALTY COUNTS

If one of my mother's employees fucked up, she was very direct and told them—but that didn't mean they were off the team. She would always give them a chance to improve and prove they were loyal to her and to the club.

I remember one night the intercom went off in my mother's office and it was one of the girls freaking out that she couldn't go onstage. A lot of the performers working in my mother's clubs were transsexuals, and the tape this girl was using to "tuck" her male genitalia had broken, and she didn't have any extra tape backstage. My mother was running around, trying to keep the show going, and was frustrated at the performer's lack of preparedness, so she barked back, "You better fix it and get out onstage immediately—even if you have to superglue your dick to yourself!"

Unfortunately the performer did not get my mother's sarcastic sense of humor and did exactly what she suggested! Later, when she was done for the night, she realized she couldn't get the glue off and started freaking out. After my mother told her what a fool she was for actually gluing her genitalia, she sprang into action and called the superglue company to see what could be used to remove it. My mother felt terrible that the girl had done this to herself, but she was impressed by her sense of dedication.

A few years later, the girl went to my mother and asked for help to pay for her surgeries to become a woman, which my mother gave to her because of her loyalty.

Proving yourself to higher-ups

As an employee, you want to show your boss you're an asset to the business. I said "asset"—not ass kisser. The last thing you want to do is pay your boss some lame lip service. Trust me, I have had lots of people try and suck up to me, and it sets my teeth on edge.

One time a stylist came up to me backstage at a hair show and started telling me about how "amazing" I was onstage. It didn't take long for me to realize the guy was completely bullshitting me and hadn't even watched a minute of the show. When I called him out on it, he looked mortified. Don't try to fake-compliment me. It doesn't work. He would have been better off telling me how upset he was that he had missed the show. Maybe then I wouldn't have told him to piss off.

If you want to get your boss's attention for all the right reasons, then . . .

• Be reliable. Every boss wants an employee they can count on. Even when shit happens, don't crack under pressure. Prove yourself to be a go-to person.

• Be accountable. No lame excuses. If you screwed up, come clean. I want to hear what you did, why you did it, and how it won't happen again.

• Take charge. Ask to oversee and help new hires; support your coworkers or spearhead a new project. Show me initiative, and I'll show you an employee who's going places.

• Make my life easy. Pick up after yourself; deal with small problems so I don't have to; think about how you can best support me and the business.

Tabatha's Final Take:
Own Your Work Relationships

✳ Great employees are created through great leadership. Be the boss who makes her expectations clear and demands quality and commitment of herself/himself and others.

✳ Hire the best people by asking the right questions and listening to the responses.

✳ Live by the same rules that apply to your staff—or lose their respect.

✳ Reward hard work and dedication with praise, acknowledgment, and compensation.

✳ Continually educate your staff so they can become better at what they do.

PART IV

Own Your Challenges

11

Reputation

• •

"I probably don't care quite as much as I should about what people think of me personally, but I do care about my reputation. What's the difference? Your reputation is how you are widely regarded—the things people might say about you when your name comes up. A good reputation can save your ass, and a bad one can haunt you for life."

• •

Not long ago I was asked to go on a national talk show. For the piece, I needed to show the host what goes into cutting and styling a client's hair and have the host try it. The show wanted to film in a salon that was in New York City, close to the studio, and asked me to choose the location. I suggested someone whom I thought would enjoy participating in the show, and he was more than happy to accommodate the film crew for a couple of hours. I even made sure the crew shot exteriors of his signage so he would get some exposure in the episode. The filming went well, and I thanked the owner and left. It's important to note that these shoots require confidentiality because the producers don't want it to leak before they are ready to promote the show that week.

The following morning I got an e-mail from a friend: "Nice mention on Page Six!" I truly had no idea what she was talking about until I saw the piece. It had details that you had to be there to know. Was it a bad piece? No, but it still made me furious. I certainly would never want to get the reputation for being a blabbermouth or a publicity whore. The segment hadn't aired, and I didn't want the production team to think I was responsible. I called the salon owner, who gave me various excuses until he finally admitted that his PR company leaked it to the press. Luckily the show understood it wasn't me who had loose lips. But it taught me a valuable lesson about guarding my reputation. A reputation is a very fragile thing, and it's not always something you can control. But you can Own It. You can focus on feeding and growing your reputation until it serves you well.

Unlike your brand, which you can have some control over shaping, your reputation is created by others, through word of mouth. It's a part of your identity that is defined by others.

People talk; you can't stop them. I wish I could tell you that it doesn't matter. I wish we could all just simply do our best and not have to worry about public opinion. But if you intend to be any kind of success in life or in business, your reputation matters and must be golden. Who wants to work for a company that has a lousy rep? Who wants to hire someone who is widely regarded as lazy, selfish, or dishonest? We have all seen someone's great reputation go up in flames after a poor choice (several politicians and Hollywood actors come to mind). It's naïve to think that a reputation doesn't affect your future success, especially in this day and age, when word travels faster than the speed of light via social media and the Internet. What makes your reputation so difficult to maintain is that it is not solely based on your behavior but rather on how others interpret that behavior.

If you're a person who craves control (like me), this isn't easy to swallow. But it's a fact and something we all have to face. Try not to think of it as high school, where everyone is judging you. Instead, be true to who you are and make sure that integrity shines through in everything you do. A lot of people get into trouble with their reputations when they stray too far from their authentic selves. Suddenly they are doing things that are not appropriate or are perceived as wrong for who they are. A politician should not have an affair. A professional athlete should be a role model and not do drugs.

A GOOD REPUTATION VS. A BAD REPUTATION

A good reputation . . .

Takes many good deeds to build.

Can't be forged overnight.

Is earned by saying the right things
and following up with actions.

Takes work to maintain.

A bad reputation . . .

Takes just one bad deed to earn.

Requires no time.

Is earned by saying the wrong things
and following up with actions.

Can take years to erase.

Building your reputation, step by step

Wouldn't it be nice if you could simply post on Facebook: "I'm a good person! Like me!" and earn yourself a solid reputation and rabid following? But it isn't that easy. A reputation takes work. You have to grow it and be consistent with your strategies.

You are who you associate with.

So find yourself people with a good reputation and emulate them. What is it that makes them trustworthy and relatable? What is it that people respond to? Hang out with losers and dirtbags, and you'll become known as "one of the gang." Simple as that.

Don't trash others.

It may make you feel like a big shot, but it's only projecting that you're insecure, petty, and weak. To have a positive rep, you need to be a positive person. If you have nothing nice to say about someone, keep your mouth shut.

Prove you're responsible.

People with good reputations continually show that they are reliable, capable, and trustworthy. Volunteer for tasks—even small ones—and make sure you follow through on them. Drop the ball, and your reputation will go down the toilet.

Make contact.

You can't have a good reputation if no one knows who you are. Get involved in social activities and reach out to the people in your professional and community circles. You know what people with good reputations all have in common? A shitload of friends and supporters.

Mind Your Own Business: What's my rep?

Need to gauge how people view you? Take this quiz, answer honestly, then check your answers below.

1. *Your boss is pregnant. You know this because . . .*

    A. she told you (and you told everyone else).

    B. everyone is whispering (but you hate gossip).

    C. she told you she might need you to take on more responsibility in about nine months.

2. *When it comes to friends . . .*

    A. the more the merrier!

    B. you think friendship is overrated; you have a cat.

    C. you have a loyal circle of best pals who you can rely on.

3. *Your local church is holding a fund-raiser for the holidays. You . . .*

    A. offer to publicize it through your Facebook page, Twitter, Instagram.

    B. will be the last one they call. They probably don't even have your number.

    C. will volunteer to do whatever they need.

4. *Your neighbor has a new litter of puppies. She . . .*

    A. asks you if you will spread the word and help her find people to adopt them.

    B. doesn't ring your bell—you rarely answer anyway.

    C. gives you one as a gift—she knows you would never say no.

5. *Your sister is getting divorced. She . . .*

A. asks you to throw her a "coming out" party and invite all your cute single male friends.

B. sends you a change of address card—with her maiden name.

C. trusts you will hold her hand through the ugly court battle.

If you answered *mostly a's*: You have a reputation for being the blabbermouth on the block. Gossip Girl's got nothing on you. It's great to be gregarious and you're the go-to person when there is any info that needs to be broadcast to your large social circle. The downside? People might think twice about trusting you. They naturally suspect in-your-ear is out-your-mouth—and they might be right.

If you answered *mostly b's*: You have a reputation for being a loner. Being regarded as a recluse is not going to win you any points in your professional or personal life. My suggestion: break out of your shell. Try making a few friends (and I don't mean online) and spend some time practicing your social skills. Not only will you feel better, but you'll also increase your worth in everyone's eyes.

If you answered *mostly c's*: Tried-and-true is your reputation. People know that you are a solid citizen and loyal friend that they can count on. My only caution: don't allow yourself to be a pushover. If people know you'll always say yes, they will dump as many tasks on you as you will take. It's okay to say no if you truly don't have the time. No one will think less of you.

One of the most important ways for a business to ensure it has a good reputation is to follow the customer reviews. If you don't know what your clientele is saying about you then you can't fix it. I went in to help a gay club in California that had been around for a long time. Not only had the club been around a long time, but so had the rules. And as the club fell on hard times, the owners became less and less hospitable to their clientele. The rules became more important than actual customer service. And they had the reviews to prove it. Many of the reviews I shared with the owners accused them of being cheap and mean. That reputation was not helping them keep longtime customers or win over new ones. To make matters worse, the owners weren't even aware of these reviews or their reputation. Luckily, once I brought it to their attention, they sprang into action and agreed to change. But if the owners had continued to be unaware of the issues that people were talking about and had not addressed those issues, then it would have been a killer—for both their reputation and their business.

Your world wide web

I love social media. It's a great way of connecting with people and finding out what people are talking about. It keeps you up-to-date about what is happening in the zeitgeist. It can be an invaluable business tool, a way to promote your business and reach people who otherwise you may have never been able to reach. It can also be a curse if it isn't used wisely. Case in point: a woman I know had a thriving design business. She made clothes for businesswomen that could easily be transformed from day to night. Her clients were steady and loyal, until one day she started posting details about her impending divorce. She asked if anyone could fix her up on a date;

if anyone had a killer divorce attorney; if there were any great bars in the Meatpacking District in New York where she might land a new man.

Her Facebook page became a series of rants about her ex instead of a way to promote her spring line. Fast-forward a year: her divorce is final, and her business is finito. I can't say I was surprised. She single-handedly trashed her reputation by turning her social media into a place to vent. Her clients didn't want to hear it, and it was highly inappropriate. Unfortunately she was seduced by the fact that she had a captive audience of more than twenty thousand followers. She never once considered the damage she might be doing to her reputation or to her business.

Social media is all about creating interest and engaging people. As a business owner, this can help you drive traffic to your Web site or blog or even to your front door. If you are concerned with growing a positive reputation, it can give you a voice and a following. There was a time when I didn't know a tweet from a pin, and I had never even heard of a hashtag. Setting up your social media from scratch can seem daunting. What I advise you is this: get comfortable with one tool (such as Twitter, Facebook, Tumblr, Myspace, Pinterest) before you delve into more. Set up an account and post a few things. See what resonates with people. Remember that anything you post is out there; you can't take it back, even if you delete it. Someone will have seen it.

Also understand that the essence of social media is communicating to a network of strangers as well as your friends. It's important to be smart and cybersafe and steer clear of scams and predators. I'm not being paranoid; I'm being careful—and there's a big difference.

• **Don't spill too much.** Your profile page has a place for address, phone number, date of birth, and other personal info. You don't need to fill it in—unless you want to open your home up to potential stalkers and identity thieves.

• **Create a tough password.** The first four letters of your last name or the numbers 1234 are not it. Come up with something no one would guess, and don't post it anywhere. It's also not a great idea to have the same password for multiple accounts—for example, your ATM password should not be the same as your Facebook password. And if you suspect you might have been hacked, change it immediately.

• **No financial deets.** Never post a checking account or credit card number or even send it over e-mail (it could be hacked). Some scams look pretty convincing, such as, "Please click this link to update your account information." Chances on they're not from eBay, PayPal, or your bank. This is called phishing. If you suspect this might be a "spoof e-mail" trying to get your personal information, then call the official number or check the Web site for how to forward suspected fraud. Never, I repeat, never click on a link that asks you to supply your info. Don't fall for it.

• **Leave out your whereabouts.** I would never tell my FB followers where and when I was planning on going on holiday. Save the photos and bragging rights for when you return. If you have a large following, this is like extending an open invitation to a burglar.

• **Never post anything you wouldn't want a future employer to see.** Because trust me, once it's out there, it's out there. A quick Google search can find all your past indiscretions (the topless pic you tweeted from South Beach; the photos of you drunk at a frat party). I know we all do crazy things, but you don't have to advertise them.

• Keep your business site all-business. While we all enjoy a good Twitter rant or indulgent selfie, there is no room for that when it comes to your business. Make sure your employees understand that you will not tolerate inappropriate postings or unsolicited opinions.

Norma's Notes: I AM WHO I AM

People think their reputation is something that is purely external, characteristics we project and how we want to be seen by others. When I was young, I would complain about how intimidating my mother was to me and to other people. My mother would just smile and say you can only be intimidated if you allow yourself to be intimidated. I never quite understood that until I got older and people would tell me how intimidating I was, even though that was not my express intention in the situation. Sometimes people who are intimidating can get a bad reputation. They may be called difficult, or in my case a "bitch." My mother knew exactly what her reputation was, and she was fine with it. Some people thought she was tough or cold, but she was very fair and had a moral compass that she lived by without exception, which is more than I can say for a lot of people. In the end, the only person any of us really answer to in terms of who we are and how we behave is ourselves. So no matter what your reputation, remember, you have to live with yourself. Can you?

Tabatha's Final Take: Owning Your Reputation

✳ It takes years to build a good reputation . . . and minutes to create a bad one.

✳ Your reputation is not solely based on your behavior but rather on how others interpret that behavior.

✳ Prove your reputation with responsible acts and staying above the fray. No need to trash people to make yourself appear better.

✳ Use social media as a smart tool to grow your contacts and reputation. Just don't get too personal: don't share any deets you wouldn't want the whole world to know.

12

Competition

· ·

"I come from a competitive family. Two of my brothers are champion athletes, so I grew up knowing what winning looked like. I saw what was required to take home the trophies and medals. I understood the hard work, dedication, sweat, sacrifice, passion, and tears that went in to it. It taught me that dedication and hard work pay off and that competition can light a fire inside you."

· ·

I began my television career on *Shear Genius,* a competitive hairdressing show. I can honestly say that while I was competing with everyone on that show, I was mostly competing with myself—and there is no fiercer competitor than me. I hold myself to a high standard, and I challenge myself to always be better and always raise the bar. Some people shy away from competition—I know quite a few who break out in hives at the mere thought of confrontation. Others thrive on it—even if it's just a game of Words with Friends, they *must* win. Competitiveness does have a bad rep. If you look it up in the dictionary, it's synonymous with words like *combativeness* and *aggression.*

But if you ask my opinion (and you're reading this book, so you are!), a little healthy competition never hurt anyone. Where would the world be without rivals? Whether in history (Kennedy vs. Nixon; Elizabeth I vs. Mary Queen of Scots) or in fantasy (Harry Potter vs. Voldemort; Luke Skywalker vs. Darth Vader), face-offs are a fact of life. Bill Gates once said, "Your school may have done away with winners and losers, but life has not."

Today it's no secret that when one company creates a new phone, MP3 player, or computer, another company releases an even "better" one a few weeks later. Why? Because competition is a kick in the ass. It's a great motivator and a way to incentivize us all to try harder. It encourages us to take chances, try new things, and push the envelope. It can drive innovation because it inspires us to look at things differently and more creatively. It helps us focus on and commit to what we need to improve to succeed. In business, if there weren't competitors, we would become complacent and take our customers and employees for granted. And you know where that gets you . . . nowhere fast.

CASE STUDY
The salon that needed incentivizing

I worked with a salon that had terrible retail sales. The owner and I both knew that increasing this revenue stream was a key factor in saving the business. Only a handful of stylists even offered their clients products; the majority felt uncomfortable "selling." They told me "we aren't salespeople, and our clients don't want us to push product on them." I pointed out that clients actually want to keep their hair looking good after a service and see this as a worthwhile investment. I suggested to the owner that the best way to incentivize the stylists was to have a little contest. The stylist who sold the most retail would win $100. Suddenly, it was game on! Once they started to engage, the stylists were surprised that clients not only welcomed their recommendations, but that they also appreciated them. At the end of the day, they hit their goal to increase sales while pleasing their clients. And that is a win-win.

Competition is everywhere: in school, in athletics, in business, in politics. Someone has to win and someone has to lose—that's what makes the world go round. But there is a big difference between healthy and unhealthy competition. When you own your competition, you understand that this is not about beating someone up so you can revel in being better or bigger. It's about pushing yourself to achieve your very best. Even if I didn't win *Shear Genius,* I won because I advanced my career in a whole new direction. There was a bigger personal prize for me than just bragging rights.

When you don't own it, competition turns into a pissing contest or World War III. Trust me: you've seen it in action. Just go to a kids' soccer match or baseball game and take a look at what's happening on the sidelines. Check out the pouting, screaming, and even name-calling. Mind you, these are the adults I am talking about—not the children! Because their sole focus is on winning, they have removed the fun, the team spirit, and the healthy competition from the game. They have replaced it with envy, anger, or resentment. You can't own your competition if you let it take you to a dark place. This side of rivalry brings out your worst and can destroy everything you've worked so hard to achieve.

You also need to make sure that you are motivated to compete for the right reasons. When I first came to the United States, I felt like a duck out of water. I didn't fit in or look like any of the other girls I worked with. I didn't have that "shiny factor" as I like to call it: the perfect teeth, body, long hair, and boobs. I felt like I had to compete, even though deep down, I didn't want to be like them. So I succumbed to that feeling and decided to get breast implants. It all went terribly wrong and turned into multiple correctional surgeries and being sick for a very long time, but it taught me a valuable lesson. When you don't own your competition, you allow it to feed your insecurities. You feel like you are not skinny enough, young enough, rich enough, successful enough—the list of "enoughs" is endless. Healthy competition should drive you forward and prove your strength and determination. It should never push you into doing something that is not truly you.

HEALTHY VS. UNHEALTHY COMPETITION

Healthy competition . . .

encourages you to push yourself harder, dream bigger, achieve more.
challenges what you think you are capable of.

requires you to take risks, be creative, stretch your limits.

makes you feel good about yourself—win or lose—for trying.

Unhealthy competition . . .

encourages you to feel envious or resentful over
someone else's success.

can make you seek out competitors who are weaker—so
you have the upper hand.

might motivate you to "play dirty" so you can beat your rivals.

makes you feel sad, angry, or unworthy when you lose or fail.

• •

Competing with yourself

I'll admit, I have a long history of competing—it definitely lights
a fire in me. When I was younger I was extremely overweight. Although I have a handle on it now, it was a struggle my whole life.
When I was a teenager and trying to diet, my mother and I decided
to do it together, as she had some pounds to shed also. It was a great,
supportive idea, but it backfired because she had a much easier time
dropping the pounds than I did. At every weekly check-in, I felt like
I was a loser, but not the one I wanted to be! When I got older one of
the things that actually helped me drop the pounds and get healthy
was competing, but this time not with Mom, but with myself. Instead of setting a goal that seemed insurmountable, I would tell myself, If you lose two pounds this week and walk twenty minutes
every day you can have a piece of chocolate." I would then get on the
treadmill, get to my twenty minutes, and then challenge myself, Bet
you can go ten more minutes. On and on this competitiveness went
until I could do an hour or more and eventually added weights. My
weight dropped, and I met my weight-loss goal. My inner opponent
does a great job of kicking my ass.

When you stop comparing yourself to others and focus on yourself, amazing things happen. You let go of all the negativity, anxiety,
and ill will. You focus on becoming a better, stronger you, and you
take control of your life. True competition lies within. Believe this

and let it be your driving force. Measure your success on your own terms and pledge to be better than the person you were the day before and the day before that.

Mind Your Own Business: **Words of wisdom**

Sometimes we need a reminder of what we're doing and why we're doing it. I have a lot of favorite quotes that motivate me. I jot them down when I see them. Collect your own, then live by them.

- "Act as if it were impossible to fail and it will be."
- "Don't count the days, make the days count."
- "She who does not hope to win has already lost."
- "If you are good, be better."
- "Losers let it happen, winners make it happen."
- "The minute you quit is the moment you fail."
- "Go hard or go home."

What if you lose?

It happens. The best and brightest don't always win, and sometimes cheaters are rewarded with victory. No one likes to lose—that's why they call it "the agony of defeat." But how you handle loss is what matters.

- **Skip the pity party.** Wallowing will get you nowhere. Lick your wounds then move on.

• See it as a temporary setback. One loss does not a loser make. Don't let it shake your confidence.

• Consider why you lost. I know that doing a "postmortem" when you feel like crap is the last thing you want to do. But it must be done. Was your opponent stronger, smarter, more prepared? What can you do to arm yourself better next time?

• Now nip it in the bud. Don't let one loss snowball into a string of them. Change your approach and your strategy.

• Losing does not define you. For that matter, neither does winning. Keep things in perspective.

• Losing makes you tougher. No one gets to be a ballbuster (not even me) without being beaten down a couple of times.

• The path to victory is littered with losses. As I have said before, no one is an overnight success. Everyone has suffered their share of setbacks—they just don't publicize them. Chalk this one up as one of yours.

Norma's Notes:
THE PASSION BEHIND THE VICTORY

My mother didn't believe in empty competition. She believed in excelling at what you loved. When she was young, my mother loved to ballroom dance because it got her away from her difficult mother and it was a way to meet boys. For these reasons, she took pleasure in dancing and therefore took it seriously and became accomplished at it. And eventually she became a champion ballroom dancer in Australia. But she didn't compete at dancing for the sake of winning; she won at dancing because it was something she loved to do. This is an important lesson for me. I don't compete at anything for just the sake of competing. That is a waste of time and energy. I don't have any desire to sit and stare at some trophy mantel. And people who do may not value those trophies in the same way as someone who truly loves what they have done to earn them. I have a passion for hairdressing and have won many accolades. But they don't mean something because I beat other people; they mean something because they validate what I love to do. So be competitive but do it for the right reasons, because winning in and of itself can be very empty.

Tabatha's Final Take: Own Your Competition

✳ Competition can be a great thing if you allow it to inspire and motivate you. You should always strive to be bigger and better. Only asses sit on their asses.

✳ Be wary of what is behind your desire to win. Is it achieving a personal best or beating the shit out of someone you envy?

✳ Don't be afraid to lose. No one wins all the time. It's the losses that make you appreciate the victory even more.

✳ Sometimes you can be your own best opponent. Push yourself beyond your limitations and see your potential. Stop comparing yourself to others, and just worry about what you need to do to be the best you.

13

Decisions

. . . .

"I am not going to lie to you: life is filled with tough choices, both personal and professional. Not making a choice, letting fear or doubt hold you back, is the only sure way I know to fail."

. . . .

One of my mother's greatest fears was getting cancer. So when she was eighty years old and diagnosed with Stage IV cancer, she was genuinely freaked out. The doctor told me it was terminal, and I had to make a decision about whether to tell her or not. I was worried that if she knew the truth, she would give up right then and there. I decided that it would be better for her if she believed she could beat it. She was a tough, stubborn woman. If she thought there was a chance, she would be fierce.

So I told her she was going to have chemo treatments and then she would be okay. In the beginning, she believed me and stayed motivated and felt healthy. But eventually the treatments had an adverse reaction. As she got sicker, she never asked and I never told her what was happening or why. She came to terms with it herself in her own time. This may not be the right decision for other people in a similar situation. But I don't believe there is always a clear-cut "right" or "wrong" in certain circumstances. There is only what feels right to you. The important thing is to be decisive and stand by your decisions when the going gets tough. This is what owning your decisions is all about. In my case, it was a very hard decision to make, but I wouldn't change it if I could.

Life is driven by decision making, and you can't live in fear of making the wrong ones. If you try to avoid decisions, you become paralyzed. And frankly, as you'll learn in the next chapter, even mistakes are opportunities to learn. So if you do make a decision that takes you off course, you need to look at it as an opportunity to grow and then figure out how to get back on track.

CASE STUDY
The Mexican café
that served waffles

Indecision is the biggest threat to a small business because in order to build success you need to make tough choices all the time. Recently I met an owner of a Mexican café who could never quite make up her mind—about anything. The restaurant's name led customers to believe it was a sweets shop, but when they came through the door, the decor had a Moroccan flavor. To confuse customers further, the menu had 101 items—everything from pancakes and smoothies to ham-and-cheese sandwiches and Chinese chicken salad. It gave customers a headache just trying to read the damn thing, much less to figure out what to order! I suggested that the owner solve her identity crisis by focusing on what she was actually passionate about. She was from Mexico City, her chef specialized in Spanish food, and her customers loved her tacos. The answer seemed clear: zero in on what you know and what you do best—Mexican food. Tacos, quesadillas, and a couple of great salads were all she needed to build a successful business. And once she made that decision, everything else fell into place. She renamed the business, retailored the menu, and the customers came running. Mission accomplished.

Some people prefer to defer decision making to the alignment of the stars or asking a Magic 8 Ball for a solution. While I enjoy a good psychic reading, I believe you need to be in control of your decisions. I don't care what your tarot cards are telling you, it's your choice and no one else's. How many times has a loved one or boss asked you to make a decision only to later tell you that it's not what they would have done? Well then, they should have made the decision in the first place and not delegated it to you. We all need to own our choices and make them with eyes and mind wide-open. Do your homework; gather your research; get your professional opinions and advice. Then take a deep breath and decide WTF you want to do. The very act is empowering; it gets you unstuck and let's you take charge. I own my choices, the good ones and the bad ones, and I can live with them. Why? Because I am in control.

Mind Your Own Business: How to make the right choices

I don't say it's simple; there are many things to weigh. Which is why I want you to make a decision—a small one, a big one, it's up to you. Before you do, write down the following. It will help you get into the habit of not just pulling the trigger. You'll actually think through each choice and calculate what's involved. Consider:

*   Your goals. Before you make the choice, what is your objective? What do you hope will happen and what will be the best possible outcome? When you know this, it's much easier to weigh the pros and cons.

*   The consequences. Now what are some plausible outcomes of your decision not going according to plan? Can you live with them?

*   The people it will affect. Will your choices have a ripple effect—either good or bad—on those close to you?

*   Is the decision really "you"? Is it true to your passion, your vision, your values?

*   Are you making a decision because you are feeling overly emotional? Are you doing something rash because you are angry, upset, or too excited? Decisions made in haste are often reactionary instead of proactive.

*   What your gut is telling you. While I don't recommend making a decision in an overly emotional moment, I do think you need to follow your instincts. Intuition is an important tool when it comes to decision making. Consider it closely.

Drown out doubt

So now you have a clear process for making a decision, but you are still struggling. A little voice inside your head keeps nagging away at you, saying:

"What if?"

Everyone who is faced with a major decision is bound to worry about the worst-case scenarios. Your mind races as you picture all the possible bad outcomes of your choice. You want to be assertive, but something keeps nagging at you, and you think, What if I'm making the wrong decision? What if I fail? You know what I say to that? What if you're not, and what if you don't? You will never know the answers to these questions unless you go for it. Don't let self-doubt become an excuse for not trying.

"Is it worth the risk?"

I find it useful to write down every risk, every element that could go wrong. Look at the list and honestly assess how likely it is that any or all of those things will happen. Try not to be a pessimist. Be realistic about whether these risks are real or are a figment of your self-doubt. Then ask yourself if all of the positives, including your passion, outweigh a lot of these issues. If you can live with the outcomes you have listed, if they don't physically harm you or leave you destitute on the street, then you can make the decision to forge ahead, knowing that you truly assessed the pros and cons.

"The timing isn't ideal."

Is it ever? Do you ever truly know when it's the right opportunity and the right moment for you to do something? You're busy, you're stressed, you're struggling to make ends meet, you're about to get married and then you're about to have a kid. . . . I hear you. Life is filled with complications—today and six months from today. If you wait for life to stop throwing you curveballs, you will die waiting. There will never be a "perfect" time to change your life. Make your choices here and now—not tomorrow or the day after. A dream deferred is not a dream come true.

CASE STUDY
My decision not to delay

I put together the plan for my salon, got the SBA loan, signed the lease, and was getting ready to open when 9/11 happened. The suburban town in New Jersey where I was opening was hit very hard by the tragedy, and the entire economy came to a grinding halt. A lot of people in my life thought I was crazy and warned me that it would be a terrible time to open a business. They strongly urged me to wait and not take the risk. But in the end, I believed in my business and in myself. I did it anyway, because I felt there was a need for my services, in spite of such a huge tragedy. And yes, it was hard to open at that time, but I built a steady and loyal clientele, and my salon was a success for many years.

"I don't know WTF I'm doing."
Knowledge is your greatest asset and will help you feel confident in your decision-making process. Before you make a decision, arm

yourself with all the info you need. But in addition to gathering information and doing your research, you should also look to your own experience. Your past experiences are a great guide to successful decision making because you have been there and done that. You can draw on what has or hasn't worked in the past.

"People say I'm crazy . . ."

I know I don't seem like the type to care what people think, but in certain instances, I do. Feedback is critical to successful decision making, and I always invite questions and critiques when I'm faced with a big decision. Refusing to listen to doubters is a surefire way to miss opportunities for improved decisions. That said, if you believe the person is just a naysayer, then their feedback needs to be taken with a grain of salt.

Excuses, excuses

Excuses are the most insidious success killer. Trust me, I have heard them all. People make excuses because they don't want to take responsibility for their decisions. It feels easier to make an excuse about why something has gone wrong than to take responsibility for it and then have to face fixing it. I can't tell you how many times over the last few years a failing business owner has told me the problem is the economy. And my response to that is always the same: "I'm good, but I'm not that good. I can't fix the economy, so I guess I'll leave." Inevitably the owner is scared of the truth, which is that they have made bad decisions and now they have to face the music and fix them. The bad economy has affected every business. But if you can't find ways to scale down and stay in business, there are probably some things that need to be fixed internally. In order to make decisions effectively, you have to wipe out all the excuses and get to the heart of what is really going on.

CASE STUDY
The froyo owner who had bad taste

I worked with an owner of a frozen yogurt shop who was in complete denial about the poor quality of the product she was selling. She told me the frozen yogurt was delicious, but when I made her try it, she struggled to deny that it tasted sour. Then she went into excuse mode. It was her staff's fault for not cleaning the machines properly. It was the machine's fault because they were bought used. "Really?" I asked her. "And who made the decision to buy the used machines and to hire the staff? Whose responsibility is it to train the staff and make sure they clean the machines?" Initially she tried to blame the machines on her husband and the training on her manager. My final question to her before I was ready to get up and walk out: "Who owns this business?" There was only one answer to that question. And finally she realized she needed to stop making excuses and start taking responsibility for decisions.

Norma's Notes: THE RIGHT CHOICE

It's okay to cut yourself some slack when something emotionally taxing happens. Allow yourself the time and space to make a decision, and then you will make the right one.

Sometimes you are capable of only making an interim decision, but that's okay because, hopefully, it allows you the time and perspective to make a larger and more permanent decision down the road. When my mother found out that my father was having an affair, she had a decision to make. Would she stay or would she go? Like many women faced with this decision, she had to factor in sharing a business and livelihood with him and having a child to raise. Ultimately my mother came up with her own unique solution—as only she could do. She decided to share my father with his mistress. He would split his week between our house and the mistress's. In my view, this was not a positive decision. And in retrospect, I think she did it out of fear and financial necessity. But what the situation ultimately showed her is that she was actually happier and better off during the time when he was not there. And eventually that empowered her to make a bigger decision, which was that she didn't need him anymore. I think a lot of women can relate to this. When they first find out their spouse is cheating it feels like the world has ended. This may not be the time to make life-changing decisions. But with some perspective they can start to see all the ways in which they didn't need this person, and they may even realize they'd be better off without that person.

Tabatha's Final Take: Own Your Decisions

⁎ Weigh each decision you make carefully. What are your
   goals? What will be the impact? Consider the fallout and
   the possibility of failure. Can you live with them? Then
   the decision is the right one for you at this place and
   time.

⁎ Don't let doubt paralyze you. There will always be
   reasons not to make a choice and plenty of people
   who will try to discourage you. Owning your decisions
   means drowning out the voices that hold you back.

⁎ Take responsibility for your decisions. No excuses; no
   passing the blame if it doesn't go according to plan.
   Know that you always have the opportunity to get
   back on track and learn from your mistakes.

14

Mistakes

. . . .

"To be honest, when it comes to mistakes, I am not very forgiving of myself. Because my job is to show people what they're doing wrong and how to fix it, I hold myself to very high standards. I want to be a good example and I get pissed off when I screw up."

. . . .

Mistakes are messy, and no one likes dealing with them—myself included. I'm a perfectionist; I expect the best and nothing less from people, and that includes yours truly. I am my own worst critic and I set very high expectations for myself.

No one likes to admit they're careless, sloppy, forgetful, ignorant, or plain out wrong. The important thing is to learn from your mistake so you do it differently next time. I'll be honest: this chapter was a bitch for me to write. It isn't fun to consider how I've screwed up. Mistakes can be a major confidence killer. We're taught from grade school on that a mistake means you're doing something wrong—like when you make a mistake on your math equation and fail your algebra test. We are conditioned to be ashamed of our mistakes and to shun them. But part of Owning It is learning how to face your mistakes head-on and handle them. What can you take away from this negative experience that will help you grow?

I know you've made mistakes in the past and you're going to make them in the future. So let's own that fact and build upon it. I want you to suck it up and do the work this chapter requires. Think about how your reaction to mistakes affects your life. When I make a mistake, I scream, I curse, and then I channel that reaction into action. Be honest: how do you feel and deal? I find that most people react in one of these three ways:

• **I feel stupid.** "I could kick myself for being such a fuckup." In my opinion, regret is a waste of your time and energy. Pity parties don't fly with me. When you make a mistake, have a moment of self-loathing, then let it go. Owning your mistakes doesn't mean beating yourself up for making a poor choice. It means acknowledging that there are better choices you could have made, admitting My bad!, and learning from them so you can move on to bigger and better things. Every mistake is an opportunity to do it better next time. Never let your mistakes defeat you or demoralize you.

• **I feel angry.** "I am furious that this happened! Heads are gonna roll . . ." Bitch, bitch, bitch. Do you think that's going to fix the problem? No, so allow yourself a moment to blow off some steam, then put aside the anger and get to work figuring out how to be productive and fix the problem.

• **I'm surprised.** "This isn't my fault! I had no idea this was happening." Hello, Miss/Mr. Denial. Of course you knew; you just chose not to see it. No one likes to hold up a mirror to his/her imperfections. But it's not just necessary; it's invaluable. When I help a business that is in trouble, I point out mistakes they have made, and most of the time they are recognizing them for the first time.

Mind Your Own Business:
Oops, I did it again!

Owning your mistakes is key to avoiding them in the future. I want you to be totally honest here. If the following happened, how would you handle it? Choose a or b, then evaluate your answers.

1. *The electric bill was due four weeks ago . . . and you forgot to pay it. Now you're in the dark. You:*

   A. call the power company and bitch them out. How dare they do this?

   B. march your ass down and pay it pronto—and set up an automatic monthly payment plan through your bank.

2. *You forgot it was your best friend's birthday and blew her off for drinks after work. You:*

   A. make up an excuse: your great-granny is in the hospital and you had to visit her instead.

   B. call and apologize and send her a belated birthday gift.

3. *Your desk is a mess and you've misplaced an important report for work. You:*

   A. tell your boss someone must have stolen it off your desk and accuse your cubicle mate.

   B. clean up your act! Organize your space so this doesn't happen again.

4. *You ordered the wrong products. You:*

   A. tell the vendor it's his fault and he should send you new ones right away at no charge.

B. admit you made an error and ask if there is a way to exchange them ASAP.

5. *You told your employee it was okay to take off tomorrow for a doctor's appointment—but you realize you need her. You:*

A. threaten to ax her if she doesn't come in.

B. explain the oversight and ask her if there is any way she can reschedule, or ask another staff member if she can fill in.

If you answered *mostly a's*: It's time to come down off that high horse and be accountable. You can't keep blaming everyone for your slipups. Take a good, hard look at how you react when something goes wrong. Screaming, complaining, and passing the buck are not smart strategies.

If you answered *mostly b's*: You understand that owning your mistakes allows you to take control of your life. When you screw up, you take immediate action to fix it. This is what Owning It is all about!

CASE STUDY
The boss who passed the buck

I met a salon owner who was driving her own business into the ground with obsessive couponing and discounting. She didn't give a damn about the quality of the work; she just wanted to pack in more clients and keep moving them in and out of chairs. As a result, the cuts and styles were sloppy, her clients were in tears, and no one was coming back. She wasn't running a salon; she was running an assembly line!

I saw immediately that this was a huge mistake, but she kept insisting that all was well. When it came to her salon, she had blinders on. Every time I pointed out what was wrong, she told me it was working. She would throw her staff under the bus at every turn when all they wanted was a leader who was consistent and honest, and a reasonable work flow where they weren't giving away their work.

"The stylists are lazy, and the customers don't know what they were talking about," she told me. Because she constantly and openly passed the blame, her problems snowballed. Unhappy clients didn't appreciate being told they were wrong, and her staff kept quitting because they felt abused. Even though she said she "got it," she refused to change her ways. This owner's inability to see her own mistakes was the cause of her own failure.

Who, me?

Lying to yourself and/or to others about what you did and why you did it is not going to make a problem go away. Neither is pretending it never happened. When you ignore a mistake, it only gets bigger. Don't dig yourself into a hole you can't get out of. My pet peeve is people who are in denial of their own mistakes yet love to pin the blame on someone else. It's like the kid who hands his friend the rock and points to the window. But when his friend breaks the window, he points the finger and says: "It wasn't me! It was him!"

If you own your own business, the mistake—even if instigated by someone under you—falls squarely on your shoulders. I don't want to hear that you're not to blame. If you are losing clients because your staff is rude, then it's your fault for not reprimanding them or setting a better example. If the sandwich you're selling is stale because your manager didn't stock the kitchen properly, ultimately you are responsible to that unhappy customer. Your employees may make mistakes that you would never make, but if you allow them to happen and go unchanged, the mistake is as much yours as it is theirs.

I can't tell you how often I ask the owners of failing businesses if they think their employees are doing a good job, and they assure me that they are. But when I show them footage of what has gone on in their absence, they are always stunned at the staff's unprofessional behavior. I've learned not to be surprised by these revelations. More often than not, a big part of why these businesses are failing is because the owner has no idea what is going on, because they have chosen not to see the mistakes that the staff are making—which is, in fact, the owner's biggest mistake!

There are many ways to spot mistakes and to stay vigilant; the choice is yours. One suggestion I make to owners is to walk into their business as a new customer or client. Experience your business for the "first time" and see what you spot with that fresh and critical eye. I have been known to send in "secret shoppers" to get their reactions to specific aspects of a business. You will discover mistakes that you had no idea you were making. Sometimes owners decide to use surveillance cameras to unearth mistakes being made in their business. Unless you suspect theft or other illegal activity, I would strongly suggest you communicate with your staff about these cameras. They can drive a wedge of distrust between you and your employees if they are not dealt with in a transparent and productive way.

ASK AWAY!

A brief customer survey is a great way to assess how your business is doing and to unearth mistakes. You want to keep it short (this isn't an exam!) and easy—no more than a few questions. Ask your customer if they wouldn't mind filling it out, and stress how important feedback is. A great motivator is the chance to win a free service or product in a monthly drawing. That usually gets a lot of customers to fill out a card! A lot of businesses offer multiple choice or scales that clients simply check off. I think open-ended questions are a better way to gauge how satisfying the service was. For example: "What improvements would you like to see in our salon?" or "How can we better serve you?" Some businesses ask if they can e-mail clients a survey—it's less intimidating if you're not responding on the spot and have time to think.

Once you have your answers, look them over objectively. Is there an issue that customers are consistently pointing out (such as no toilet paper in the bathrooms, slow waitstaff)? These are the things you should tackle immediately. I also recommend leaving a line for general suggestions. Often customers come up with brilliant ideas for how to grow your business. They're the ones patronizing you after all; they know best what the public wants and is willing to pay for.

The nine most common mistakes business owners make

Yes, making some mistakes is par for the course when you own a business. But that doesn't mean you shouldn't try your damnedest to avoid screwups. Save yourself and your customers the headache! Here are some of the most common mistakes I've encountered in troubled businesses and suggestions on how you can sidestep them:

1. **Failing to set policies.** Put a process in place for your business to help it function smoothly and efficiently. Define your policies, everything from what you expect of your staff and how you want your customers greeted to how you want the place cleaned and stocked. You should have everything clearly set forth in writing, including how people will be held accountable.

2. **Failing to follow through.** Many owners drop the ball on maintaining rules and standards. Sometimes it's because they are overwhelmed and forget. Other times it's because they can't be bothered. This sends the wrong message to your staff and your customers about you and your business. You don't want people to think you're a pushover or inconsistent.

3. **Failing to plan for the future.** What will happen if the market suddenly changes, if someone quits, if a new competitor moves into the neighborhood, or if you outgrow your current space? As an owner, you need to be thinking about the future of your business and how you can protect it, grow it, and adapt to the current marketplace.

4. Failing to communicate. As an owner you must always communicate clearly with your staff. They can't read your mind. Don't assume they know what you want or what they should do unless you tell them clearly. Part of good communication is consistency. You can't say one thing one day and another the next. You can't have different rules for yourself or some employees and not others.

5. Failing to reprimand staff. As an owner, you can't be afraid to be the bad guy. Being a strong leader means being clear when your staff has done something wrong. Tell them what they've done and how to fix it. Don't raise your voice or curse. Communicate in a calm and professional manner.

6. Failing to manage money. We all know you need money to open a business, and you need money to keep it open. We talked about this in chapter 5. As a general rule: know what's coming in and what's going out.

7. Failing to be open to change. Owners need to be adaptable and flexible. If something isn't working, change it. Don't just hang on to a bad idea because you are lazy or don't want to admit you were wrong.

8. Failing to prioritize. As an owner, you will wear many hats and spin lots of plates. Prioritize what is most important and needs to get done for your business to succeed. Oversee this yourself and delegate the less important tasks to a qualified employee.

9. Failing to take responsibility. Owners often say they opened their business because they wanted to be their own boss. But being your own boss doesn't mean sitting back and relaxing while everyone else does your dirty work. In fact, when you

own your own business, you work even harder than when you work for someone else. The responsibility for your business's success or failure is yours.

Mind Your Own Business: Make a "shit might happen" list

I like to do this exercise with people starting a new business venture—it's a great way to troubleshoot any future problems. Basically you're going to brainstorm potential mistakes you and/or your staff might make in the future. Be brutally honest: Where could you possibly screw up? What could go wrong if all hell broke loose? Then talk through how you would handle it. What if the cappuccino machine breaks down—do you have a backup plan? What if you overbook several clients at once? How can you set up a scheduling system that will prevent this? You are proactively avoiding these mistakes by anticipating them ahead of time. No one likes to imagine the "what-ifs," but it gives you greater peace of mind knowing you have a plan to handle them.

Keep moving on

I have seen a lot of people "stall" in life or business because they couldn't deal with the fact that they had made a mistake. They couldn't get past the notion that things hadn't gone 100 percent according to plan, and so they came to a standstill. Dwelling on your mistakes only holds you back. It keeps you feeling stuck, helpless, lost, even depressed. Are you going to sit on your ass and sulk, or are you going to correct the problem and rise above it? I'm very tough on people who can't own up to their mistakes. To be successful, you need to try your best, take risks, fall down, and pick yourself up again. I expect it of you; I expect it of me. I hate a defeatist attitude. I truly believe there is almost no problem so big that you can't find a solution and work hard to fix it. You can take tremendous pride in turning a bad situation around—it shows strength, leadership, and the ability to achieve great things.

Even if your ego is a little bruised, remember that you're not a failure unless you let yourself be one. Keep in mind my four *A*'s when it comes to moving past your mistakes:

Acknowledge it. "I did it."
Assure yourself. "I screwed up, but I can fix it and I'll survive."
Act to fix it. "I'll do my best to remedy the situation and move on."
Avoid doing it again. "I see what I did wrong and why, and I'm not going to let it happen again."

Norma's Notes:
"NEVER LET THE TURKEYS GET YOU DOWN"
This was one of my mother's favorite expressions. She was my biggest fan and thought I rarely made mistakes. But as I get older and reflect back, I can see plenty of instances where I did

screw up. I know that she was trying to tell me to "get over it and keep going." And that is probably one of the best lessons she ever instilled in me. I always dust myself off and plow ahead. It is the only way to succeed. So I might amend her saying slightly: "Never let the turkeys get you down . . . even when you are the turkey."

Tabatha's Final Take: Own Your Mistakes

✳ Don't beat yourself up for screwing up. Embrace your mistakes to learn what to do and what not to do in your business.

✳ Admitting you were wrong won't make people respect or like you any less. Quite the opposite! Once you set that example, your staff won't be afraid to own their mistakes and learn from them.

✳ If you believe you never make mistakes, then you are not being hard enough on yourself. Go back and reread this chapter! If you are afraid to make a mistake, then you will probably never live up to your full potential.

✳ With every mistake, you should grow, change, and make yourself better. That said, you should make any mistake only once. If you don't learn from your mistakes, you are doomed to repeat them.

15

Well-being

. . . .

"All work and no play can make anyone (even me!) a less effective owner. I've always believed you need to take time to recharge your batteries to be at your best every day."

. . . .

I am lucky that I have always loved what I do—so even when it is really hard work, I usually love it. But everyone has their limits, and you want to avoid hitting the wall, because that doesn't benefit anyone. When I opened my own salon, I worked seven days a week and came in at all hours to satisfy my clients. With this kind of schedule, I started to realize I wasn't loving work quite as much. I was exhausted, and I was setting an unrealistic example for my staff. It took me a while to figure out that I was actually shooting myself in the foot by working *too* hard and not recharging. I couldn't be a good boss when I was running on empty.

I still struggle with balance, as do many of us. Investing in your personal life can feel selfish and indulgent. But you have to understand, you're not "goofing off" or letting people down. You are actually allowing yourself to be a better friend, partner, coworker, boss, even parent. What good are you if you are overstressed and overworked? You become:

- more likely to make mistakes.

- unable to solve problems efficiently.

- slower and less productive.

- quicker to snap, lose your temper, or forget things. (Ever notice how your car keys go missing when you're frazzled?)

Finding the right balance between business and pleasure is about setting boundaries, prioritizing, organizing, and learning to manage your time. Sometimes that means saying no to an obligation or favor that you usually try to fulfill. It's not easy saying no to a friend or family member, but in this instance, saying no doesn't make you a bad person. In fact, you are doing it so you can be a better person for everyone. And sometimes you need to say no to work obligations that you would typically meet because you are overextended.

When I traveled internationally for a major product company, I would often fly for twenty-four hours to reach my destination— then get right to work. As part of my job representing the company in other territories, I felt compelled to go to all of the social events the host invited me to. But the grueling schedule was taking its toll, and I was miserable. So I started saying no. And you know what happened? Nothing! The world kept spinning, and nobody thought any less of me for asserting myself.

When I film my show I disappear for months at a time. I am so focused and busy that I fall off the planet. I have had to have conversations with friends: "I'm working. It doesn't mean I don't care about you, I just have a priority right now—which is my job."

Are some of them annoyed? Sure. Do I feel bad that sometimes I miss personal events? Absolutely. But when you own your well-being, you know you're making the right decisions for you *right now.*

The scale may tip and you won't always strike that perfect balance, but you are confident that your choices are coming from the right place. At any given moment, I can tell you my priorities: what needs to be attended to immediately; what can go on the back burner. Sometimes "me time" is at the top of that list; sometimes it's at the bottom. This balance is different for every person, and you need to find yours.

Recharging for me is not a scheduled event. It's on an as-needed basis. I know when I feel tired, unfocused, and have a shorter fuse than normal. Sometimes that break is just an indulgent pajama day watching TV, reading, staying home, and cooking. Other times it's taking five minutes for a cup of tea and a mental shutdown. I like to be busy, so if I am "off" for too long I get twitchy and need to be stimulated. There are a lot of ways to recharge, depending on the situation:

- Take a mental health day and do something just for yourself, like get a massage, go to a movie, or stay in bed all day.

- Take a vacation and go someplace you have always dreamed of or get away to someplace you know relaxes you.

- Treat yourself to something you have been wanting as a reward for your hard work. It might be a shopping trip to Alexander McQueen, but it could also be something that isn't expensive but just as special.

- Engage in physical activity that you enjoy. Recommit to the gym or hire a trainer to help you stay on a program. Reconvene with nature by taking hikes. Or maybe set a new personal goal, like running next year's marathon.

- Give back. Do something special for someone in your life, surprise them with your generosity. Or volunteer to do charity work and give back to the community.

- My personal favorite is cake day. My mother and I shared this one. One day a week eat whatever you want!

The company you keep

One of the most important things you can do is surround yourself with people who support you and understand what you do, both at home and at work. Sometimes I am with my colleagues more than my family, so I need to have people on my team who share the same values and work ethic as I do. This creates an important safety net for me, because I can take a time-out, knowing I can count on those people to hold down the fort. A trusted staff will help you feel confident about stepping away for your me time. And when it comes to my loved ones, they often need to be patient with how much time and attention I give to my work. Part of balancing your work life and your personal life is choosing the people who will support both and allow you to find that balance.

CASE STUDY
The hubby who blew off his business

I once worked with an owner and his wife. Although her husband was the "boss," he wasn't always present at the salon and spent a lot of time pursuing his other interests. He was philanthropic and helped his church with various missions. At one point he left his business and his family for six months to do church work. While this may seem noble, it left his wife to work long hours to keep money coming in, and she very rarely took time off from the business. All the staff acknowledged that she was the hardest worker. She would often come in at 6:00 A.M. and work straight through till 11:00 P.M. to accommodate her clients. When I met her, she was exhausted mentally and emotionally. She wasn't even sure she wanted to be a hairdresser anymore! When we talked, it became clear to me that she loved what she did, but the pressure was getting to her, and she felt burned out. When I confronted her husband about the situation, he was shocked because he thought her love of the business was carrying the burden he left her with. I explained that he needed to step up and be in his business full-time. And he acknowledged that his wife was entitled to some time off for good behavior. When I checked back in on them weeks later, she was a different woman! She was spending time with her kids, taking time for herself, and had even picked up old hobbies that she loved. And their relationship had become more of a healthy partnership—which was also helping their business become more successful.

Open your eyes and prioritize

There will always be times when you are faced with conflicting demands that can't all be managed at the same time. It's unavoidable, no matter how much you plan and prepare. And when it happens, it's tough to know which obligation to meet first and which one to let go by the wayside. You will have to prioritize what can wait and what can't.

Case in point: in the salon industry, certain times of the week and year (such as weekends and holidays) are busier than others. From early November to the beginning of January, my salon was packed. And I knew this was a great opportunity to work a lot of hours and make a lot of money. I also knew that my staff wanted time off to spend with family and friends. So I made it clear ahead of time: we would be working long hours, and there was no time off. But everyone would get a break when things slowed down and the holidays were behind us. Because we shared the same goals, for the most part my staff wanted to take advantage of the season to make money as well. There might have been a few whines, but we pulled together and worked our asses off.

Finding the right combination of work and play isn't impossible. It takes effort and maybe a bit of paperwork (I am a person who writes everything down). A few of my suggestions:

• **Everything works better with a schedule.** You need to pencil into your calendar your personal activities along with your business appointments. Include your kids' soccer games, or date night with the spouse. Not only does this give them importance and relevance, but it also allows you to see where and when you need more balance.

• **I love lists** (see "my daily 'to do' list" below). They help me stay organized, on top of what I need to do, and in control. Writing everything down and listing what needs to get done and when is a great way to see where you have time that may be better served.

• **If you don't prioritize, someone else will.** They'll invade your time, your turf, and your boundaries because you haven't set them.

• **Don't allow other people to dictate your balance.** Your priorities are yours alone. If you worry that you will disappoint others or hurt their feelings, you will never be in control. Just make sure you communicate your priorities to the people in your life so you can manage your expectations.

• Know your purpose and your passion. This will make prioritizing easy. What do you want out of life? Sometimes a personal engagement will be more important to you, and sometimes it will be work.

Mind Your Own Business: My daily "to do" list

Some days it feels like I have way too much on my plate. That's when I make my list and check it twice. It gives me a sense of calm and control. Start by asking yourself, What needs my immediate attention? Is it a work deadline? An early-morning presentation? A meeting with your kid's kindergarten teacher? Then assign a timeline to your tasks, from most urgent to least. That way you manage your time and see clearly when things can get accomplished. If it's a large task, try to break it down into smaller, achievable steps to make it less daunting and more manageable.

Consider your short-term and long-term goals. Maybe there is no pending deadline on restocking the shelves at work, but if one of your goals is to grow your product sales, then it should be a priority. Finally, refer back to your list during the day and check off tasks as you complete them. Nothing gives you a greater sense of accomplishment!

CASE STUDY
The owner who couldn't
get her act together

One of the most important aspects of finding balance between your work life and your personal life is feeling in control of both. Stress at work can give you sleepless nights or worse. And as I always say, it is a disaster when you bring your personal problems to work.

I worked with an owner in New Jersey who was so disorganized it was lucky her head was screwed on or she would have lost it. Her salon was failing, and she was deeply depressed over it, including having severe insomnia. Her physical condition was no doubt also contributing to how scattered she was at work. She had no idea where anything was, including her checkbook. Her bills were all over the place, stored in shoe boxes or plastic bags with no system at all. No wonder she was always late paying them! When I asked her to produce a bill or receipt, all she could do was rummage through the chaos. Her excuse was that she didn't have an office. While that was an issue, it went much deeper than that. She simply didn't want to deal with the financial situation of her business because it was too depressing. But she was losing important documents, being charged late fees, and even losing track of personal appointments. So I gave her homework: "Take this mess home and organize it. Sort through the boxes and bags and prioritize." When she did, she felt in control for the first time in a long time and actually slept better than she had in months. That was the first step she needed to take to get herself back on track. In the year or more since I worked with this owner, she has been sleeping every night, lost over thirty pounds, looks great, and feels great. And, by the way, her business is now going strong.

How to have a life (not just a career)

It's easy for me to tell you "Get a life!" but how does one actually do that? It starts with taking care of yourself in some way, whether that is mind, body, or soul. I know how difficult it is to carve out time during a busy workday, but it's one thing you can't sacrifice. You don't have to take vacations or even days off to start balancing work life and personal life. Start with five minutes a day and build up as your schedule allows. Here are some ways to get started.

• **Learn something new.** In your spare time, take a class, read a book. It can be motivating and invigorating and can get your creative juices flowing. It can also benefit your business while nourishing you personally. I had been very stressed at work and was searching for something that would help me relieve that stress but also focus my energy. So I decided to try Transcendental Meditation. I hadn't really meditated before, nor do I practice yoga. But TM seemed like a potential solution to the personal and professional issues that I was having at that time, so I let myself be open to it and what it could do for me.

• **Eat well and exercise.** This seems obvious, but it's usually the first thing that goes out the window when you're stressed and busy. When I came off the road after one of the seasons of my show, I was not feeling well physically and was really run-down. I went to see a doctor, who implemented a whole new healthful diet for me. Sometimes when I got lazy or stressed I didn't follow it, and then I felt like crap. So now I am careful to take the time and energy to eat well.

• Get organized. If you have let things get out of hand, sit down and get your act together. Disorganization is a sign of depression or a loss of control. Start with something concrete, like your kitchen drawers or your personal files, and use the process of getting organized to motivate you to take charge.

• Don't take your work home with you. That is not to say you won't have to do work at home sometimes. I mean this more as a state of mind. You need some time in the evening to recharge for the next day, so put the work aside for a nice meal with friends or family or an hour at the gym or in front of the TV. You need some you time.

• Remind yourself every day to *breathe*. You'd be surprised how sedentary we all get. Try focusing on your breathing a few times throughout the day. Take a walk around the office to get the blood flowing.

• We all spend a lot of time in our offices, so you need to recharge yourself there as well. Freshen up your work environment. Sometimes a fresh coat of paint, moving things around, or revamping your retail area is a huge morale boost for you and your staff. When you feel great about your space, you'll look forward to coming to work.

Norma's Notes:

ONE DAY A WEEK WAS OUR DAY

My mother worked incredibly long hours when I was a kid. I remember there were many days she worked through the night and got home at 5:00 A.M. No matter how tired she was, she was always up in the morning to make me breakfast and drive me to school. It was at the top of her daily priority list. She also made sure Saturdays were Our Days. We would have lunch at a fancy restaurant and catch up on what was going on with school. She was a successful businesswoman, but I never felt neglected. She showed me you can balance your personal life with work. That doesn't mean you literally divide your time fifty-fifty. It just means that the time you make for yourself or your family is quality.

Tabatha's Final Take: Own Your Well-being

❋ As much as you want to give 110 percent to your career, you need to also make time for yourself. All work and no play is a recipe for stress, and no one likes a dull, cranky coworker or boss.

❋ Organizing is the ultimate way to take control. A cluttered desk and a messy bag filled with everything but the kitchen sink will leave you feeling lost and confused.

❋ The only way to make room in your schedule for everything is to prioritize. What needs to be done at this moment? What can wait? No guilt or apologies! This is what you want and need. If someone can't understand that, they can piss off (or come see me!).

❋ Schedule in at least five minutes a day for you and you alone. It can be a quiet coffee break or a chance to power nap. If you feel there is nothing in your life but your work, explore new areas and hobbies.

16

Changes

· ·

"I've always been a David Bowie fan and I think I know why: 'Ch-ch-ch-changes! Time to make the change!' For my generation of club goers, Bowie represented fearlessness. You could look like anything and be anyone and you could still be spectacular. This is what everyone needs to internalize, because change isn't easy . . . or wanted . . . or at times even expected. But it is inevitable."

· ·

Y ou can't make time stand still, and you can't prevent transitions from happening. What you can do is face them with dignity, grace, and strength. This is owning change, in every sense of the word.

Look at the music industry. I am certainly not the first to point this out, but record companies resisted digital distribution. They "tuned out" Steve Jobs and iTunes. But change was inevitable and it was their demise because they didn't embrace it. A great album used to be a license to print money, and it made careers. Now, no one cares about an album. It's all about the single and it's all about the viral distribution of the video of the single. Labels now play the game and "release" things early online to gain traction in the market. Look at white female rappers. What? Who? They write and record their own songs, film their own video, launch it on You-

Tube, and have a million views by lunchtime. Look at Lil Debbie or V-Nasty or Oh Blimey—yes, these are real recording artists. They are owning their own careers and monetizing them because the traditional record industry didn't embrace the changes.

So if Capitol Records can't embrace change, how will you? The good news is, any large, established industry is slower to recognize and embrace a new trend than an individual, as long as you are open to seeing it. So why is personal change difficult? Because it can unsettle our sense of identity. Change makes us rethink everything we've thought was certain, dependable, and reliable up until this point. Even good changes can cause stress: a promotion, a wedding, a pregnancy. Suddenly you find yourself thinking, Oh, shit! Nothing is going to be the same as it was before.

You are right, but the key is not to frame change as negative. You need to see change as an opportunity. You need to remind yourself of all the transitions you've dealt with successfully in the past: starting a new school, landing your first job, bouncing back from a breakup. Regardless of whether a change is negative or positive, it is an opportunity to grow. You are moving from one phase to another; one step to the next. You need to think of this as progress. Onward and upward from here . . .

CASE STUDY
My move to TV

I decided that I wanted to do my own TV show because it would grow my career and my brand. But I had to think about how it would affect my business and my home life. I had to deal with my staff's anxiety, and I had to prepare for being away from my salon. I had to make sure my mother was okay and set up the home front. It was pretty daunting, but the possibilities made it worth it. In the end, nothing in my business or home situation went horribly awry. But I could have used my fear and hesitation as an excuse not to make the change. There would never have been a TV show. So I'm glad I embraced this new phase of my life (and I hope you are, too!).

When change sucks

Not every change is positive. I get that. You're getting divorced, you got fired, you lost a valued relationship. Even these changes have a way of giving us a much-needed kick in the ass. Change can be an amazing catalyst, even if we don't recognize it at first. Here's a perfect example: a friend of mine lost her father. It was sudden and tragic. She actually had a conflicted relationship with him because he was unhappy in his life, and they had come to an impasse.

She felt guilty and conflicted when he died, but ultimately it helped her take stock. She decided that life is too short to waste. She gave up a job that did not fulfill her and pursued her dream to become a doctor. The loss of her father was a tragedy, but it inspired her to reevaluate her own choices and make a major change. She rekindled a relationship with her mother that had drifted and remade her family. Ten years later, she recalls the moment she lost her father as one of the most impactful in her life—the one that brought about the most positive changes she had ever made. Would she have done this if she hadn't experienced that loss? Maybe not. Some changes we make, and others are made for us. But the positive end result can be the same if you Own It.

Let's face it, some changes are outside of your control and you are forced to adapt. If you have to deal with a change that isn't yours, regroup. The people who adapt the fastest to change are those who are able to refocus. Gather your resources, summon your courage, and stay on course. You can react to the imposed changes by making changes of your own, but first you need to take stock, assess, and make a plan. Act, don't react.

HOW TO DEAL WITH CHANGE

- Allow yourself time and space to reflect on the change that is before you. Don't let others rush you to a decision. This is your own process, and you need to own it.
- Talk to others who have been in your shoes. A support system is key for any transition. You can benefit from their experiences.
- See yourself in your new situation. Envision how you want things to go and then make a plan for how to execute that change.
- Look at the context. Your boss was fired and someone new has come in. They aren't firing you and you don't know what their goals are. Speak with your new boss and lay out your expectations and ask him if they are in line with his.

- Be the best version of yourself. In any kind of transition, positive or negative, it can be challenging to get your bearings and showcase your best traits and skills. But it is essential that you do this. Rise to the occasion.

Ultimately change is good for all of us. It forces us to reassess where we are and where we are going. And it requires us to adapt, which means we are growing. If you aren't willing to change, you are in stasis, and that is deadly. Think about the restaurant that hasn't redecorated in twenty years. You avoid it, even if the food is still good, because you feel like it is "tired" and "behind." What about the boyfriend with whom you have sat on the couch and watched the same shows for years? Ho-hum. And he may change it up before you do! You need to think about the aspects of your life that have stalled and challenge yourself to change and keep it fresh. Otherwise, you will be left in the dust!

Norma's Notes: NEVER LOOK BACK

My mother was fearless when it came to change. Look at how she had to adapt when my father left. When we moved to London, it was a pure adventure. I was training at Sassoon and she was working as a nanny. Some might say we had no idea what our future held and others might say the world was our oyster. And when my mother moved to the United States for a man she was dating, she had no idea how it would turn out. But she leapt off the cliff willingly. My mother taught me that change is always good, if for no other reason than it means forward motion. And, of course, that means you never look back. There can't be regrets when you embrace change. Even if you think the way things were was better than the way things are, you need to continue to look forward. Keep changing until you find the right place.

Tabatha's Final Take: Own Your Changes

* Not all changes are under your control—but how you handle them is.

* See change as an opportunity, not an obstacle. You are moving from one phase to another, and this is progress.

* Successful people adapt fast to change. They don't react; they act.

* Change forces you to reassess where you are and where you are going. This is a good thing, so don't be afraid of it!

CONCLUSION:
OWN IT ALL!

Congratulations, you've made it! The keys are within your reach. But let's take a moment to review and regroup. If you have actively engaged with this book, then you've learned how to take ownership of your life from every angle. There is no situation, no challenge, and no decision that you can't handle. In a nutshell, it all comes back to this:

- Make a plan and let it evolve.
- Don't be afraid of decisions, even tough ones.
- Learn from your mistakes, and then move on.
- Teach people how to treat you.
- Treat people how you want to be treated.

The most basic principle of this book and how I live my life is to always man up, step to the plate—you can choose your metaphor here. It all boils down to: Own It! Ownership comes with responsibility. Owning your business, owning your life, owning your relationships: you shouldn't expect it to be easy. But then again, to use the cliché, nothing worthwhile comes easily.

Think back to a moment when you were embarrassed, even mortified, about something. You would have preferred to crawl under a rock or jump out the window rather than admit any part of it. But when you owned up to it, you realized it wasn't so bad after all. The relief of Owning It far outweighed the consequences. This is a rule in life. You are always better off Owning It, even when Owning It seems brutally hard.

I ripped off a Band-Aid when I came out to my mother. I sat down one afternoon and told her that I was living with my girlfriend. My mother had a hard time with this news and refused to speak to me for almost a year. Of course I had moments of doubt during that icy time, and I even wished I hadn't told her the truth. But the alternative was not acceptable. I would have had to continue to lie to her about who I was. Eventually my mother realized exactly that, and she respected me for my choice not to lie. She respected me for owning who I am. The outcome was worth all those difficult months, because as a result of them we were closer than ever. Also, because I could embrace this change in my life completely, I was happier than I had ever been.

Mind you, I am aware that sometimes you come out to a loved one and they never get past it and the relationship ends. But I would argue that you are still better off owning the truth and being proud of who you are than living a lie and hiding.

Owning It is fundamentally about being proud of who you are and what you do, even when you are not perfect, even when you need to make changes. So the point of this book has been to help you feel strong and empowered enough to own all aspects of yourself, even the imperfect ones. Remember, we should always be changing and improving. And Owning It will help us with this process.

So take your keys, unlock the future, and step through. These are the keys to the kingdom, so use them wisely and remember, I may be back. . . .

APPENDIX

ask TABATHA

People are always asking me questions—and not just about business. I get everything from "Where did you get those kick-ass shoes?" to "How do I find a new 'do that will make me look thinner?" I'm always happy to give my opinion (be prepared: I will tell you what I think, and it may not be what you want to hear). So when I put out the word that I was seeking questions for my book, I was flooded with a lot of great ones. I couldn't possibly answer them all, but I did my best to give you a good assortment. If you have any other questions, feel free to reach out to me on Facebook or Twitter, and I'll do my best to answer if I can!

BUSINESS WORRIES

I owned a small toy store for several years. It did well at first, but people are now buying toys cheaper on the Internet. What can I do to get customers back?

I think this is a problem that a lot of businesses are finding now. Cybershopping is fast and easy; you don't have to leave your home and many sites offer steep discounts and free shipping to sweeten the deal. But what they can't offer is the experience of going into a store and gazing at the shelves in search of something special for someone special. The solution for you is to promote your business in the right way. You want to reach parents who are looking for that personal touch. You can guarantee they will get individual attention in selecting the perfect gift for their child or someone else's.

I think someone on my staff lied about his experience. He told me he had worked as a short-order chef in a diner, but his food is either burned or undercooked, and my customers are complaining. How do I handle this?

When you're going through the hiring process, make sure that you're not just taking someone's word on his experience. He can write anything he wants to on a résumé—did you even follow up with references? Did you have him come in for a short trial period to make sure his work was up to par? Now you'll know better for next time. But in the meantime, you're faced with an employee who is falling short. Sit down with him and go through your expectations, your policies, your procedures, and the way that you want things done in your business. Make sure he gets the training he needs to follow through with your requirements. If he wants to please you, help him do so.

My husband and I owned a bar in our neighborhood for ten years. We just got divorced and the last thing I want to do is work with him! What am I supposed I do?

Any time you go into business with a family member, a partner, or a best friend, something that you always need to think about is an exit strategy. What's going to happen if the relationship goes wrong or your life changes and you decide you don't want to be in the partnership anymore? Your situation is tough, because you had that emotional tie. But you have to look at it from a nonemotional point of view. If you want to get out of the business, is your partner going to pay you your share of what it's worth, or can you afford to buy him out? Can you afford to go out and start again? If the answer to these questions is no, I don't see any other choice. You have to put the personal aside and work together and come up with some sort of strategy to keep the business alive.

I own a café, and the people who work for me are idiots. I'm sick and tired of them screwing everything up! Why do I have such bad luck hiring waitstaff?

Well, that's a great question and something that you really need to sit down and ask yourself. You know where I stand on this: it all goes back to the boss. If you're consistently finding that your staff isn't up to par, I suspect you're responsible for the problem. Are you being clear with what you expect of your team? Are those expectations reasonable? Are you communicating effectively with them? Are you hiring people who don't have the training, the qualifications, or the personality that you want to be in your business? As an owner, you need to reevaluate what you're doing or what you're not doing to make sure you're hiring the right people. Be honest with yourself and you will find your own answer.

I think one of my salespeople is stealing money out of the register. We've been coming up short for several weeks now, and I noticed one girl has bought some new clothes and bags. I feel bad accusing her, but what if she is guilty?

I'm sorry to tell you that you've left yourself open to this situation. You need a better system in place to keep track of your finances. If your register is always coming up short, you either need to supervise it yourself or have a system so that you know every transaction that's coming in and out of that cash drawer and who's making them. If you do suspect that someone is stealing from you, keep a close eye. Take him or her off cash register duties immediately and make sure they're supervised. Don't accuse unless you're 100 percent sure he or she is guilty. And if they are, I recommend you show them the door. I would never tolerate any employee who is dishonest and stealing from me.

I got angry at one of my employees and called her a fat, lazy ass. I know it was wrong, but she works for me and I write her paycheck every week!

No one wants to be spoken to in that manner and no one deserves to be—I don't care how much you think she is slacking off. It's not going to make your employee do a better job or regard you with any amount of respect. Calling someone names—especially insulting names like that—is never okay. If your employee isn't doing her job, sit her down and have a conversation about what she's not doing properly and what your expectations are. Make sure you have policies and procedures in place so that if you do need to reprimand someone or put them on probation, they understand the repercussions of not doing their job.

I'm starting a new job in an upscale showroom tomorrow. You always look so chic! What should I wear to work?

Something that you feel really, really comfortable in. The key to looking chic is to wear your clothes, not to let them wear you. So make sure that whatever outfit you choose is appropriate for the business that you're going into but also makes you feel at ease and empowered.

One of my customers asked me out on a date. He's totally hot, and I'm really tempted. No one would know . . .

Well, two people *would* know: you and the customer in question. What's more important to you: making sure the customer is kept happy and the relationship is kept professional and that your integrity remains intact, or that you give in to your libido? I would recommend never crossing this line.

I agreed to a partnership with someone who I was iffy about, but I saw a chance to be an owner and took it. Now, three years later, I've decided I want to do this on my own because my partner is very unprofessional. I am locked into a lease until 2016. I have patience, but I am growing increasingly tired of this partnership. How should I deal with this?

Lesson learned: you should have followed your gut. You had an iffy feeling in the beginning and now it's starting to show itself to you. So, unfortunately, you're in this situation and it should be a good learning experience to trust your instincts in the future. For now, you need an exit strategy. Sit down with your partner and calmly ask if there's a way that you can solve this problem before the lease is up. Are they prepared to buy you out or are you prepared to buy them out so that you can keep the business going? Be professional and fair. Chances are if your partner is behaving unprofessionally, he wants out as much as you want him out.

I think some of my coworkers are talking about me behind my back. What should I do?

My first question is: why is gossip happening in the work-place? Are you in some way (perhaps unintentionally) perpetuating it or helping to fuel it? Some people don't even realize that they like drama even as they foster it. Have you done something that would make people talk? If that's not the case (and I expect you to be honest with yourself!), you need to find out what and who is behind it. Perhaps someone is jealous of you and trying to get you in trouble? If so, the only way to deal with it is to confront that individual head-on. Maybe there is a simple misunderstanding that can be rectified. I do not recommend you ignore this feeling. If you are being singled out, then you can't allow it to spread any further.

I have completely lost my passion for hairstyling. I haven't been able to get it back except for an occasional burst over the past several years. Is it time to move on?

Only you can answer that question. You need to do some

soul-searching. Where did the passion go? What happened? Most people who say they've lost their passion are just burned out. They are overwhelmed and distracted by other things going on in their lives. They need to step away and take a break. They need to look at things differently. But if you've tried to reignite the passion, if you've tried different things to get that drive back and it isn't happening, then yes, maybe it's time to move on.

I own a restaurant in a part of the city that was once thriving but has changed. My business is suffering. What should I do?
I have taken over several businesses in areas that have changed and I won't lie to you: at times it's a big problem to tackle. Getting customers into those areas can be tough. You need to stretch your marketing outside of your area. What most people get wrong is thinking customers won't travel to them. Customers will come if it's worth the trip, and that means great food and service. I suggest talking to fellow merchants. If you feel that business has declined, they probably do, too—maybe you can team up to promote your businesses beyond the local population and even, by doing so, revitalize the area.

My boss says I need to "look more presentable." I don't usually wear makeup to work at our froyo shop, and I just throw on a T-shirt and shorts and put my hair back in a baseball hat. What's wrong with that?
You are the face of your business as much as your boss is because you are waiting on customers. I'm not saying get a blow-out every day and wear fake eyelashes. I'm saying

make some effort—especially if your boss has made a point of telling you to do so. You may not feel like it's the most glam job, but it's the job you have and you should abide by your boss's rules. Have enough self-respect to show you can make an effort.

After a decade of self-employment as a fitness professional, I am about to start a new job in environmental fund-raising and public relations. I want to look polished and professional, but I also want to fit in with my colleagues, most of whom will dress more casual for work. How do I strike the proper balance?

For me, it's looking at the situation that you're going into. I carry a pair of heels and a jacket everywhere I go, in case something happens and I'm pulled into a meeting or I need to go somewhere and meet with people. For your everyday dress (which sounds more casual), think about a great pair of jeans or pants and layering pieces together so you can take an item off or put it on if need be. Personally I never want to look overdressed, but I always make sure that I look pulled together. I am representing myself and my business everywhere I go.

I think I am too nice to my staff. How can I be tougher and more convincing if they are underperforming? This is my biggest weakness.

You can be both. Just because you're nice doesn't mean you can't tell people what your expectations are. As a business owner and a manager, the first thing you need to do is lead by example, but you also need to tell people what you expect from them so they can give it to you. Many people have a hard time differentiating between being mean and being a good leader. You need to tell people what you want and how they are going to give it to you, and then let them know when they don't deliver.

My employer put a "phone jar" in the break room with this sign: "We are trying to cut down on cell phone calls in the salon, so anyone caught on their phones has to put $1 in the jar." He's such a hypocrite! He thinks we're wasting time on our phones; meanwhile I've seen him texting on his cell phone when he's doing a client's hair!

There's nothing wrong with creating a rule that says all employees should be doing their jobs and acting professionally and productively. But if a phone jar is going to reinforce it, the owner needs to abide by the same rules. If he is always on his cell phone, he isn't leading by example. If there's a no cell-phone policy, it holds true for everyone who works in the salon—including him. Everyone has to follow the policies and the procedures. Otherwise there's no point in having them.

My husband is the one who handles all the finances for our bagel store. He recently had pneumonia, and I had to take over the books and paychecks for two weeks. I'm terrible with money, and I had no idea what I was doing! How can I can get better?

There are lots of ways to get better at it. The first is to be involved in your business! If you are an owner, you're responsible for the money as well. Even though your husband may take care of all the accounting because he's more adept at it than you, it doesn't mean you should bury your head in the sand. You need to understand the finances of your business from top to bottom. Online classes are a good solution, as is simply sitting down and talking to your husband so you learn how he runs the books. Don't wait for a health crisis; start now so you're prepared for the future. You may not love juggling figures, but it comes with the territory of being a businessowner.

I've been pet grooming for more than twenty years and have a nice, steady clientele built up. For two years I had a retail location that included mobile services, which I had to close due to high overhead. I think a combination pet grooming/doggy daycare business would be very profitable and, with my experience, very successful. How can I find someone to invest in my business with either a business loan or partnership so I can do it properly this time? I'm not able to get a small-business loan, and I don't have any family members who can help.

The first thing is put a proposal or business plan together. You need to take your idea, put it on paper, and then determine if it's more than just a good idea—if it's something that can be financially successful. When you present it to people who are potential investors, they need to know you've done your homework. If you can, give them some sort of guarantee of return on their investment. Finding investors is difficult: start with friends and family. If you have a really great idea, finding people who believe in you enough and are like-minded is the key.

I'm pregnant and due in a few months. I have my own salon, with only one employee, and all my clients keep asking when I'm coming back and how long will I be away. I have no idea how to approach their questions!

You need to approach them honestly. It's natural for your clients to ask when you're coming back because they want you to continue taking care of them. So be honest and say, "I'm going to be on maternity leave for X amount of weeks, and then I will be back." Let them know so that they can book their appointments appropriately. If you aren't honest or you lead them to believe that you're coming back sooner and don't, you will have lost their trust and possibly their business. Make sure that the employee you are leaving in charge knows what each of your clients likes and expects. Perhaps schedule a time for her to meet a few of your regulars so she can see how you style them. Assure your clients they will be in good hands until you return.

My boss is very controlling and micromanages me. I do all of my color consultations with her because she insists on it, and most of the time, instead of giving my clients what they came in for, she forcibly convinces them to get something else. When I

*challenge her or suggest another option, she yells at me right
in front of my customer. I've gotten a lot of complaints, and I'm
losing clients. What should I do?*

The biggest issue here is that you're losing clients—which
may be the key to getting through to your boss. She needs to
understand that she owns a hairdressing salon, but the stylists she has hired are creative individuals. The business is
suffering because she's not giving you the creative freedom
you need and deserve to service clients properly. If your fellow stylists are having similar problems, you know it's not a
personality conflict; it's how she's running things. That said,
as an employee you always have to understand that everything starts and ends with the owner. You can't *make* her
do something she doesn't want to do. You need to decide if
you want to play by her rules and continue to work for her.
I'd recommend that all the stylists sit down with the boss
collectively, explain how many clients you all are losing, and
talk about the things that aren't working for you. See if you
can, in a very honest, clear way, get through to her. Don't
yell; don't threaten. It's one of those situations when presentation counts. Stay calm and assure her that you are all
in this together: the client's happiness and repeat business
are paramount.

NEW BEGINNINGS

*I've always dreamed of owning my own bakeshop. I'm constantly
baking cakes, cookies, pies, and brownies for my kids' school,
and people tell me all the time that I should open a business. Am
I crazy?*

No! Not crazy at all. Some of the most successful businesses began with entrepreneurs who started their business at home and expanded into large corporations. If it's something people are praising you for and asking you to deliver, that tells you there's a market for your work that could make you some money. You already have one of the key components to success: you really love what you're doing. If you're serious about being a businessowner, work out a business and marketing plan and then do your homework. Go back and review the chapters in Part II: Owning Your Business. You need to know how to sell your baked goods, who you're going to sell them to, and how much it's going to cost you so that you can get them beyond your family and friends and into consumers' hands. Good luck!

How do I overcome the fear of starting my own business? I work in learning and development and have always wanted to work for myself, but I'm scared!

It's going to be scary. Anytime you make that kind of commitment, an element of fear is part of the process. It's fear of the unknown, of failure, and sometimes of success. What you need to understand is that you should never allow fear to paralyze you. If you do, you may never take a chance on yourself. So if you're really passionate about the business that you want to open, if you've done your homework, made your business plan, and know what it takes to actually get it open, keep it open, and make it a success, I say go for it. Put that little voice of fear on the back burner where it can't hold you back.

I am thirty-four years old and have no idea what kind of career I'm interested in. I have worked in retail for most of my life and enjoy working with people, but I need a change. Any suggestions?

Not everyone knows what they want to be when they grow up. Maybe it's taken you this long to reach a point where you're ready to find out. Read chapter 2, Passion, because that's where it starts. There must be something that gets you out of bed in the morning, something that makes you think, Even if I didn't have to make any money, I'd love to be able to do this! Tapping into what makes you happy and excited will direct you to a great new career.

I had long hair forever and recently decided I needed a change— so I cut it short. Really short. My friends think I look like a guy now. I think that's crazy—what do you think?

I think it's absolutely ridiculous that short hair is considered masculine. There are so many women with short hair who look incredibly attractive, sexy, beautiful, and feminine. So for me hair doesn't make the person; the person makes the person. If you have confidence and you can pull off short hair, then rock that style.

I have been styling hair for twenty-seven years in a salon and I am still very passionate about our industry. How can I break into freelance work?

It depends on what you mean by freelance. There are many different ways to be a freelancer. You can work for a man- ufacturer and demonstrate their products at a trade show. You can be a fashion hairdresser and style photo shoots, or work in the entertainment industry doing hair for actors in movies and television. Or you can have a private clientele. It really depends on what your freelancing aspirations are, because there are so many different options. Whatever you choose, build a portfolio of your work so people can see what you do, what your talents are, where your strengths lie, and the range of your work. You can also go to agencies that hire out freelance hairstylists as a way to get started.

I'm a forty-one-year-old woman considering cosmetology school. Am I too old to start a career in this field? Could I have a successful career at this age?

I think anyone can have a successful career at any age. It really depends on where your passions lie and how hard you want to work for them. Just because you're older doesn't mean you can't change your career path. Also, forty-one is far from ancient! Get the training and experience under your belt and you can do anything.

I've been in business since 1999, and I have moments where I say to myself, "I have no talent. What the hell am I doing styling hair?" Do you have any advice for me?

Everyone goes through times of self-doubt and lack of confidence. That's totally normal. The difference is being able to recognize those bad days or weeks and write them off as simply that. Get yourself out of that funk and move on. A lack of confidence is going to affect your work and make you start second-guessing everything that you do. You want to avoid getting trapped in that vicious cycle. What is it you want out of your career? Do you have a goal? A plan? Are you on a path to get you there? I am a huge believer in being proactive, so I am going to tell you to get off your ass and stop moping. If you want to be better at your craft, then educate yourself and practice. Lose the negative attitude and give yourself a morale makeover.

My dad has owned a hardware store for twenty years, and now he wants me and my two brothers to take it over. Here's the problem: none of us knows the first thing about running a business. I hate to disappoint my father. How can I figure this all out fast?

Well, my first question is: do you want to run a hardware store? It's always a difficult situation when a parent is getting older or ready to retire and wants to pass his or her business on. Are you ready and willing to assume this huge responsibility? If you have a passion for hardware, and you want to carry on the torch, then your dad is your best teacher. He can show you how he's made his business successful and walk you through everything you need to know. When you have a handle on it, you can then bring in your own ideas to grow the business. You won't disappoint your father by telling him you want to learn from the best—him.

My best friend wants to open a bow and barrette business with me. We think it would be a lot of fun to work together, especially doing something we both like. Do you think it's a good idea?

You have to be careful about going into business with your friends. Sure, it sounds like fun to go to work and hang out with your best friend all day long. But I warn you: when you're in business together, that's not what you'll both be doing. The decisions owners have to make can stress or even kill their relationship. Make sure you both understand this and don't make the decision lightly, just because it sounds like a blast to be in business with your buddy. If you can both promise to take on the responsibility and do the legwork necessary for a new venture, that's a good start. But I do have to caution you: I've seen many a friendship fall apart in similar situations.

I am in a dead-end mechanic job that I hate. I want to go back to school, study business, and open a car dealership. My wife thinks I'm crazy. She says I can't just change careers at thirty. We have no kids, no mortgage, so why the hell not?

I agree with you. Why the hell not? If it's something you're really passionate about and you want to advance your career, then absolutely go back and study something new and change careers. Many people change their careers two, three, or even four times in their life, and are successful each time. Just because you started out in one job doesn't mean you should stay in it forever. Your life can change, your passion can change, your path can change, and there's absolutely nothing wrong with wanting to take a different path and wanting to be successful in life.

My boss fired me (she's a bitch with an attitude), so now I'm going on interviews for other jobs. Should I lie and say I quit? Should I just leave it off my résumé?

It's never a good idea to lie because it's always going to catch up with you and bite you in the ass. You can leave it off your résumé, but you never know when you (or your new boss or coworkers) may encounter someone who worked with you at the other place. For me, honesty is always the best policy. I would sit down and look at the reason why I got fired. Is there something that maybe I could have done differently that would have ended in a different result? Was my boss truly a bitch, or was I not living up to her expectations? You can downplay the drama when you're in an interview. Be brief, don't bad-mouth your former employer, and refrain from blaming anyone else. Focus on what you learned and what you now have to offer.

I've owned two businesses before (a diner and a jewelry store), and both bombed. I want to try something new—maybe a dry cleaner? What is the secret to owning a successful business?

The secret would be to look at why the previous businesses failed. Is it because neither was something that you were passionate about? Is it because you didn't know enough to begin with? The "why" of the two previous business failures is what you need to understand before starting another business. Why a dry cleaner now—is that where your heart lies? Is that what you know a tremendous amount about? If the answer is no, I suggest you go back to square one and do your homework. Make sure the next place you open is a good fit for the neighborhood (i.e., is there a demand for it?) and is something you will put your heart, soul, and knowledge into. Your commitment is a big part of its success.

I own a Middle Eastern restaurant in New York City, and a falafel place just opened down the block. I'm worried they'll take all my business. What should I do?

Have better food than the place down the road. Competition

is actually a great thing, because it gives consumers something to compare. If you're creating a great experience with great food at a great price point, people will keep coming to you despite the new place. Step up your service: treat customers well and make sure the food is as close to perfect as possible. Look at your new competition as a way to keep growing your business and improving it. Don't let it scare you off.

I moved to a new city, and I'm currently trying to let people know about my salon. I've done all the same advertising as I did before to gain customers, such as leaflet distribution, magazines, promotions, directories, and Google, but it is simply not working. Can you please help?

Look at why it's not working and what the missing component is, especially considering that those methods worked for you before. Why aren't they working this time? I suspect it's because your approach is missing the personal touch. You need to get out there, meet people, and tell them you've just opened your business. Another great way to gain clients is to offer them a service so that they can see for themselves how great you are. Wow them, and then let them spread the word. Putting out a leaflet is not going to do anything for you. What *will* help is getting to know people and showing them what you offer and what you're going to do differently from anyone else in town. I am a big believer in connecting face-to-face—not just throwing out business cards.

Things beyond my control have rocked my world this year, to the point where my business is suffering. I have lost some clients, partially due to my issues, and I want them back. What is the best way to make amends with them and ask them to come back to my chair?

Approach them honestly and say, "I'm really sorry, I have had a rough year. I've taken some time off, I've gotten myself back together, and I can't wait to have the chance to take care of you again." Or you could tell them, "I just wanted to reach out and say I'm sorry that because I was going through some personal issues, I didn't exceed your expectations the way I did before." Let people know that you are back, that you have your shit together, and that you are going to do everything you can, not only to make amends, but to be the person that you used to be.

I have my own beauty salon at my house and I want to expand it, but my location is a huge problem. I live back in the woods, and I feel most people are intimidated to go so off the main road. Is there anything I can do to bring in more customers?

If you're doing a great job, people shouldn't feel intimidated to travel to you. If you live in a rural area, people are used to that. But since you're asking them to go out of their way, make sure you do the same. Give them great service and great value. Make sure new customers understand how to get to your home salon, where it's located, and mark it clearly with a sign in your yard. That way *you* will be on the right path.

LET'S GET PERSONAL

If you could go back and do anything differently in your business, what would you do?

I'm not really one to dwell on what I did or didn't do. I take situations and problems as they arise, face them head-on, and then work through them. I'm not the kind of person who says, "should've, would've, could've." There are probably many things I would have done differently, knowing what I know now. But making those mistakes was not detrimental to my business. They helped me grow and learn. I'm older and wiser, and yes, I would love to tell my young self a thing or two about how she screwed up. But I wouldn't waste my time or energy. It's much more effective to keep moving forward not looking backward.

Has there ever been a takeover too tough for even you to handle?
There have been lots of takeovers that have felt like they were impossible to solve, and many owners I thought I would never get through to. That's when you see me become incredibly frustrated and lose my temper. But I've made a commitment to the owner. I walk into their business to help them, no matter how tough it is or how stubborn they are. Once I've given you my word that I'm going to do something, I'm going to do it. I'll do everything I can to make sure there is some kind of positive change before I leave. But it's always left up to the owner to follow through with those changes and keep up with the success of their business. Ultimately, it's in their hands, not mine.

What has been your favorite takeover, and why?
Every takeover I do is very, very special to me. When I reflect back over five seasons, many have surprised me, so many businesses have done so incredibly well and have taken the opportunity and the experience to degrees that I never ex-

pected. These have led to unbelievable successes in businesses and personal lives, and I'm incredibly proud of all of them. But I really try not to play favorites. I always walk into a new takeover and look at it with fresh eyes. I solve the problems that business is having rather than bringing in a favorite takeover from the past or a problem that I've encountered before. I never compare; each takeover is unique and individual.

If you weren't a hairstylist, what would you be? Do you ever think you'll do something totally different with your life one day?

If I had to choose another career, it would be really hard because I love doing what I do. But if I *had* to, it would probably be a chef, because I love to cook and it would incorporate my passion for people if I ran a restaurant. But that's not going to happen! I have changed my career already. I have gone from being a hairdresser behind the chair, to owning my own business, to hosting a television show, and being a lecturer and book author. That's a lot of evolution, and I am continuing to grow my brand in many exciting directions.

I have a lot of awesome clients who bring me gifts or a tip during the holidays. I never know the proper way to say thank you. What do you recommend?

Acknowledge the client and remember to just say thank you. I always sent thank-you notes to clients as a way of reaching out to them personally. I'd write things like, "Thank you for the cookies that you baked for me. They were delicious. I really enjoyed them!" Send a note or an e-mail or make a quick phone call to show them that you appreciate the gesture.

I'm a stylist and for years I have been recommending products to my clients to use for thinning, lifeless hair. Now menopause has hit me like a ton of bricks and my hair is thinning badly. All the things I've told my clients aren't working. Help!

With any kind of hair loss or thinning, I recommend you consult a doctor to see what's going on and make sure everything's okay healthwise. Once you do that, understand that not every product is going to work for everyone. Fixing your hair problem may take a combination of things, such as seeing your physician, managing your diet and exercise program, taking vitamins and supplements, and then being gentle with your hair. No more overworking or overstyling it. Put the flat iron and curling iron away! Be patient, be proactive, and you'll get it back.

I have recently started to develop alopecia areata. I wear hats and scarves every day because my patches are getting too large to cover. Should I spend tons of money on shots and creams— or just shave my head and own it?

You need to feel confident, comfortable, and ready to be able to do that, and it isn't always necessary. There are products, hairpieces, and extensions that can improve the hairstyle you have and help camouflage the bald patches. With hair loss, it comes down to comfort. The best goal is to go about your day without feeling like you have to hide what's going on. So do what you need to get you to that place.

Do you ever allow people to hug you?

To be clear, it's not that I don't like hugs. It's that I only give hugs to people when I feel it's appropriate. I'm not the kind of person who walks around and says "I love you" if I don't. That's not who I am. I don't believe in hugs in the workplace, so when people see me on my show and I say "I don't do hugs," it's because I haven't gotten to know you yet, and I'm not going to give you that kind of physical contact. My hugs are reserved for people who I know deserve a hug or need a hug.

Have you ever been fired from a job? Why or why not?
I have always made the decision to leave a job because I felt it wasn't the right fit for me or it was time to move on and do something that would advance my career. The closest I've come to being fired was being "sold." An owner I worked for sold his business, and part of the agreement to the new owner was to sell the staff along with it so that they had full client books. I was among the staff involved in the sale, and it was very upsetting. The owner told me that if I just gave it a couple of months (because it was a requirement of the sale), I could go back to work for him. But I could never do that because I felt the loyalty wasn't there anymore.

I know you've struggled with your weight in the past. I'm overweight and working on losing it, but in the meantime I still want to look good in my clothes. Any advice would be appreciated!
I don't think any of us has a great body image, and you need to cut yourself some slack. I still struggle with my weight, and I am my own worst critic. What I have realized is that most people don't notice when I feel like I am having a fat day or skinny day. For now, choose clothes that are comfortable and flattering and make you feel good so that you can go out and face your day. Be proud of the fact that you've

made the decision to get healthier. Confidence is the best look on everyone.

Have you struggled with depression? If you did, how did you overcome it?

I think everyone has struggled with being depressed at some time or other. There's obviously a big difference between feeling blue and being clinically depressed (in that case, I recommend seeing a physician). But yes, I've had my low times, and I allow myself to feel that way. I acknowledge what has brought me to that place, and then I tell myself it's time to get on with life and move forward. I don't allow myself to wallow. What's the point? There is no good reason to stay feeling bad. Every time you pick yourself up and dust yourself off, you gain strength, wisdom, and confidence.

MONEY MATTERS

I work from home in a studio on my property, and the studio needs a few upgrades. I was thinking of opening a FundMe account, where people donate to my project's expenses and in return they will receive a percentage off services in 2014. Does it sound like I'm taking advantage of my clients? Is it tacky?

Yes, it's tacky. I think it's one thing going to friends and family members who know you and what you do and saying, "I need to expand. Would you invest?" Do it as a loan or give them a percentage of your business so that they actually invest in it and share in the revenue stream. But reaching out to clients and asking them to invest in an upgrade is poor form. You'll make them also question if your services are lacking—

since you feel a dire need for funds. Keep the relationship with your customers completely professional. If you're having money woes, it's not their problem or their business.

In every salon I have worked, I've noticed that January through March is very quiet. Now that I have my own salon, I was wondering what strategies you could recommend to increase business and money flow.

There will always be ebbs and flows in business, and specific businesses feel it even more. During slow periods you'll need creative ways to bring in customers. Research future events that are coming up during these periods: Are there any local charity events, parties, school dances, etc., that might require hairstyling? How about offering an Easter special or an early-spring highlights package? Give people a reason to need a new cut, color, or style, and they'll come running.

I work in a chain salon and I'm worried I'll never make decent money. Am I better off just building my clientele and leaving with them to a booth rental salon?

Money can be made anywhere you do a great job. While there are lots of advantages to opening your own business, there are also advantages to being a booth rental stylist, a commission stylist, and even working at a large chain salon. You need to examine what you want from your career. What are your goals, and what is your long-term plan? Do you want to be your own boss? Do you crave creativity? Or are you happier with someone else dealing with the day-to-day so you are free to service customers and hone your craft? Make these decisions first, and don't let it all be about dollars and cents.

I have been in the salon business for fourteen years, and I see that people try cheaper places or do their color at home to save money. How can I bring them back into my salon without offering coupons?

Obviously, during a bad economic climate people are going to look for ways to save money. I don't believe in discounting my work either, and I'd never advocate it, but I do believe in working with my clients and making sure that they stay in my business. Maybe there are lower-level stylists they can go to who will charge less but still give great quality. Or maybe there is a training night where you and your top stylists supervise trainees and customers pay less. Make sure you offer your clients alternatives that are price effective for them. The goal is to keep them happy and coming in the door.

What is the best way for beauty industry inventors to spread the word about their products without an advertising budget?

There are lots of ways. Going to trade shows is a good start: you'll find many salon owners who are eager to try new things. It depends a great deal on what the invention is, what testing you have done, what patents you have, and what innovations you are offering. My best advice is to visit salons and put your product in the hands of the people who are going to be using it: the stylists. They are your marketing team, the ones who will be telling people what you have to sell.

I've been doing hair for about thirteen years, and I want to better my craft. But I just don't make enough to pay for classes. Is there any way I can learn new tips and techniques for free?

Going to a hair show is always a good investment. They offer multiple classes, many of which are free after the cost of an admission ticket. You can also take online classes, plus training within the industry itself. If you reach out via e-mail or Web sites to large beauty companies, you can be kept up-to-date with the latest products and techniques. Make sure your bosses know your desire to continue your education—it's a benefit to them as well. They might be able to provide training on a regular basis. I know you don't have a lot of money to spare, but realize that if you spend it on education, you are investing in your future so you can move forward to the next level and be successful.

I own a small business, and I can't afford to hire a person to manage my social media. But everyone says it's so important. Can I do it on my own?

You can and you should. I think social media is such an invaluable tool because it's free and it's easy. Don't be intimidated. You can link social media platforms together and reach hundreds even thousands of potential clients. The sites are all very user-friendly, and there are free tools available so you can actually research numbers, look at the people following you, and the people following them. It's like a free focus group and marketing strategy all in one. Social media doesn't have to take over your life—I don't want you tweeting or posting ever five minutes! It needs to be consistent. It needs to be fun. It needs to be interactive, and it needs to be professional and informative.

ACKNOWLEDGMENTS

You know I don't say "thank you" unless it has been deserved, appreciated, and earned. That said, my heartfelt thanks go to the team of people who support me and the family and friends who love me no matter. To Lisa Sharkey, Amy Bendell, and the amazing team at HarperCollins, thank you for believing in me (again), guiding me through the process, and putting up with me!

And finally, to all of you my supporters. Without your support of me and my projects, none of this would be possible. I do appreciate you all.

ABOUT THE AUTHOR

TABATHA COFFEY is best known as the star of Bravo's *Tabatha Takes Over*, which recently completed its fifth season. She is also an author and entrepreneur. Known for her no-nonsense approach and savvy business expertise, Tabatha has been widely praised for her ability to help struggling businesses and transform people's lives. She draws on her own life experiences to offer straightforward advice and the empowering message of inner beauty and strength. Her television show, speaking appearances, and books inspire men and women around the world to take charge of their lives, their businesses, and their futures. Tabatha is featured regularly as an editorial stylist and contributing writer for fashion and beauty publications such as *People Style Watch*. Her expert advice is sought out by many television shows, including *TV Guide*. In 2011, she wrote her first book, *It's Not Really About the Hair: The Honest Truth About Life, Love, and the Business of Beauty*.